The Art of
Professional Services

Patty,

Best wishes for much success with your book.

Mary Ann
Whitemor

The Art of
Professional Services

A Guide to Integrating Services into Product Companies

Mary Ann Whiteman

Milo Hill Press
Los Gatos, California

Published by

Milo Hill Press, Los Gatos, California

Book editor: Perry Marlon
Book layout: Dorothy Foglia

Printed in the United States of America

Library of Congress Control Number: 2009929436

ISBN 978-0-615-28636-5

First Edition

Contents

Introduction   1

Part I: The Heart of Professional Services

1   Think Services   9

It's Not As Easy As It Looks
Services Are Not Products
Buying Services versus Products
Selling Services versus Products
Professional Services Defined
Not All Services Are Created Equal

2   Win the Consulting Game   25

Expertise: A Ticket to Play
Quality, Reliability, Relationships: How to Win
Trust: The Reward
Reputation: How to Play Again

3   Meet PS Challenges in a Product-Centric Environment   33

The Success Formula for Pure Consulting Firms
The Destiny of PS in Product-Centric Companies
Why Product Companies Fail Where Consulting
    Firms Succeed
IBM: The Premier Full-Service Provider

Part II: The Building Blocks of a Professional Services Organization

4   Build Plans and Strategic Alignment   **49**

Create a Business Plan
Participate in Your Company's Mission and Goals
Establish Your Fundamental Purpose and Get Buy-in
Align Financial Goals with Your Mission
Monitor and Measure Success
Corporate Resources: An Aid or a Hindrance?
PS Organizational Structure
Entrepreneur or Franchise Operation?
Questions for Consideration

5   Target Your Markets   **69**

Relationship Jeopardy: Consequences of a
     Sales-Driven Approach
For Success: A Market-Driven Approach
A Market Defined
Crossing the Chasm—for Services
Specialization: Key to Quality Control
Questions for Consideration

6   Create Your Services Portfolio   **79**

Define Your Core Competencies
Create Strategies to Reach Your Markets
Identify Your Service Offerings
Ensure Service Readiness
Aligning with Your Company's Key Products
Offering Total Solutions
Partnering with Systems Integrators
Bottom-up Approach to Service Selection
Input That Improves Your Services
Increase Customer Trust and Loyalty
Questions for Consideration

7   Adapt Marketing to Service   **97**

Organizational Dynamics
Leverage Your Company's Position
Importance of a PS Brand Image
Ensure Quality Services
Ensure Adequate Delivery Resources
Start with Marketing Basics
Build Tools to Support the Sales Team
Align Marketing Materials with the Sales Process
Make Your Consultants Stars
Turn Successes into References
What Doesn't Work
Remember: It's about People
Make It Easy to Find Your Services
Stacking Up Against the Competition
Marketing inside the Company
Questions for Consideration

8   Establish a PS Sales Force   **129**

Don't Bet on Product Salespeople
Don't Bet on Support Services Reps
Create an Overlay Sales Team
Divide and Conquer Doesn't Work
Invest in Solution Selling Training
Provide Motivation and Incentives
PS Pre-Sales Support Must "Walk the Talk"
Teamwork and Trust Between Sales and PS
Identifying Prospects
Questions for Consideration

9   Manage the Sales Process   **145**

Qualify the Opportunity
Manage the Proposal Process
Contract Management
Winning Large Deals
Questions for Consideration

10 Productize for Easier Entrée, Sale, and Delivery   161

Who Benefits from Packaged Services?
It's Not a Panacea
Choosing Services to Package
Managing the Packaged Services Process
Bundling Services with Products
Questions for Consideration

11 Optimize Services Delivery   183

Choose the Right Talent
Develop and Retain Star Performers
Motivate and Cultivate Teamwork
Implement a Skills Database
Develop Project Management Methodology
Invest in Service Delivery Methodology
Create a Solutions Database
Be Prepared to Invest
Questions for Consideration

12 Utilize Three Most Important Success Factors: Quality, Quality, Quality   203

Importance of Quality Management
Factors Affecting Service Quality
Results of Not Keeping the Service Promise
Build Quality into the Process
Learn from Your Experiences
Solicit Customer Feedback
Questions for Consideration

13 Manage Partner Relationships   223

Nature of Partnering
Partner Program Objectives
Partner Program Ownership
Building Services Partner Programs
Partner Program Pitfalls
Types of Partner Relationships
Certification for Sales and Delivery Partners
Questions for Consideration

14 Manage Business Operations **239**

Hire Experienced Leaders
Let Price Reflect Your Value
Set Pricing: T&M or Custom Quote
Match Supply with Demand
Measure Financial Performance
Automate Your PS Business Operations
Questions for Consideration

15 Bring It All Together **259**

It's about the Fundamentals
What's Unique about PS?
Uniqueness Brings Challenges
In Closing…

Bibliography **269**

Introduction

During the early years of the computer industry, hardware was king. Information technology (IT) companies sold hardware, and everything else—software, services, training, manuals—was bundled into the price of the hardware or essentially free. In 1969, the United States Department of Justice helped transform this business model by requiring IBM to unbundle, or charge separately, for each of its offerings in response to an antitrust suit. In the 1970s, other companies followed, charging for manuals, training, support, and software.

The last holdout in the move from free to fee-based work was professional services (PS)—services that utilize specialized expertise and skills to create technology or business solutions. Customers expected their hardware and software vendors to provide consultation and assistance to use their products. And if most companies provided these services for free, it certainly was difficult for any one company to charge and still remain competitive.

But gradually, high-tech companies changed the business model of professional services from *free* to *fee*. Three key factors provided the impetus for change. The first, mentioned above, was that the government pushed IBM to charge for services as part of an antitrust suit settlement in 1969. Yet it wasn't until the mid-1980s that IBM Global Services began to emerge as a real business and a significant source of revenue. The second catalyst was simply that companies could no longer afford to give away consulting services. As hardware became more and more of a commodity and the margins decreased, vendors needed to find alternative sources of revenue and to differentiate their products.

The third driving force was the complexity of the IT environment. In the early years of the IT industry, companies purchased their hardware and software from one manufacturer. The choices consisted of IBM and the "BUNCH"—Burroughs, Univac, NCR, Control Data, and Honeywell. Integrated by a single source, the products were designed to work together seamlessly. But since the mid-1980s, the IT industry has grown and diffused into many thousands of niche players with reduced compatibility. As product choices evolved at a fast pace, many companies looked to outside organizations to assist them in selecting and integrating system and application components to build custom solutions for their business needs. The pain of integration simply became so great that companies were willing to pay for professional services.

By the late 1990s, professional services became the fastest-growing area of the IT industry, and *solutions* became one of the key buzzwords. IBM's growing success in the services area stimulated considerable interest. By growing its services division into its biggest business and using it to propel a spectacular company turnaround, IBM stood out as a clear role model. To catch this wave, Compaq bought Digital Equipment Company (DEC), which had a large consulting organization. Hewlett-Packard (HP) considered buying the consulting arm of PriceWaterhouseCoopers (PwC) for $18 billion in 2001. Instead, the HP/Compaq merger in 2002 brought together two consulting organizations to form HP Services. In 2008, HP signed a deal to further grow its consulting business by acquiring EDS for $13.9 billion. In 2002, IBM acquired PwC's consulting arm for $3 billion, continuing its shift from primarily computer manufacturing into a services-led technology business.

It has become clear to many high-tech companies that integrating professional services into the product business increases product sales and provides an additional source of revenue. The challenge is how to make the move to services. Do you partner with systems integrators? Do you acquire one or more consulting firms? Do you establish your own professional services organization? If so, how do you start and grow the business?

Given professional services' short history as a revenue-producing organization in a product company, the number of managers with the know-how and experience to launch and build the business is limited. Although consulting firms, such as Deloitte & Touche and Accenture Ltd., have a much longer heritage, they do not encounter the same challenges as product-centric companies, and thus are not the best role models when building a services business in a product company. Most books about professional services describe how to become a consultant or how to start a small consulting business. Again, not what a new PS manager needs to navigate through the obstacles in a product-focused company. Without good guidance, most managers simply plunge ahead using the age-old method of trial and error.

Too often, managers assume that their knowledge of the product business enables them to lead the move into professional services. They assume that the current product infrastructure will support the services business. They struggle to find the optimal balance between centralization and decentralization within the new services organization. They are stumped by how to motivate and educate the sales organization to sell services. They apply product marketing methods and wonder why they are not successful. Many jump in and hire consultants before clearly defining their service strategies and core competencies. And some fail to meet customer expectations and lose credibility with their sales team and their target market.

Employees who transfer to PS roles from the product side of the business also face a huge learning experience. And even employees who bring a great deal of experience working for consulting firms still need to learn to tackle the challenges confronted in a product-centered environment.

When a product company commits itself to sell and deliver professional services, the need to learn new ways of doing business doesn't stop inside the walls of the PS organization. Many employees throughout the company—who know the product business—must understand the PS business in order to support it. Marketing managers must learn how to create thought leadership that builds awareness and generates leads. Sales managers must learn how to build and motivate a PS sales organization. Sales representatives must learn a consultative sales approach. Contract administrators, human resource managers, and finance managers must understand the differences between the strategies and tactics that work for products and those that produce success for services.

And, of course, the company's executive team must understand and support the PS business. In a conference for professional services managers in Silicon Valley, the main lament was "How do I demonstrate to my boss that this is a different business?" Or as one professional services manager stated, "How do I get my manager to see the 'ah-ha' about the PS business?" This book provides answers.

Whether your role is to build and manage a professional services business, work as a member of the PS team, or interface with the organization, *The Art of Professional Services* is designed to help you understand the professional services business and all the nuances of running a services organization in a product-centric company.

The book is based on my experience helping product-centric technology companies in Silicon Valley make the leap to professional services. In the early 1990s, a number of vendors were transforming their free systems-engineering services to fee-based consulting. I had the opportunity to lead that effort at Tandem Computers. After giving birth to a new PS business at Tandem, I moved to Sun Microsystems where I built a productive marketing organization for the company's new professional services business.

Shifting from product marketing to professional services, I experienced firsthand the challenges of transitioning from a product role to a services role in a product company. Many years in PS management gave me a chance to see what really produced results for a PS business—and how it differed from a product business. Working as a consultant for the past eight years, I have helped other product companies attain their professional services goals. Seeing the pitfalls and the achievements across companies large and small, I wrote *The Art of Professional Services* to share the lessons learned along the way. The book looks at the business through the eyes of a product manager—and does not assume any prior knowledge of professional services.

The book is divided into two parts:

- *Part I helps you think like a services manager.* Just as learning to play scales on a piano or chords on a guitar seems tedious when you really want to jump in and play songs, it is important to start with some basic principles about professional services. These set the foundation for a new way of thinking about business. That said, if you understand the basic principles, feel free to jump directly to Part II.

- *Part II presents strategies and operations* to build and manage a successful professional services organization. It starts with the business plan and progresses through practices to market, sell, productize, and deliver services—as well as manage partner relationships. Questions at the end of each chapter are designed to stimulate your thinking about the status of your current or planned organization and improvements needed to be successful.

The biggest hurdle that managers face in moving from products to services is the belief that they already understand the services business based on their product knowledge. The best way to start this journey is to suspend any belief that your knowledge of the product business directly applies to professional services. The issues are similar; the successful strategies and operations are distinctly different.

It is impossible for a man to learn what he thinks he already knows.
—Epictetus

Mary Ann Whiteman

PART I

The Heart of Professional Services

If your role is to build and manage a professional services business, work as a member of the PS team, or interface with the PS organization, this book will help you understand the professional services business and all the nuances of running a services organization in a product-centric company. The first step is to learn to think like a professional services manager.

A product mentality is one of the biggest stumbling blocks faced by most product companies when launching a professional services organization. Just as it is more important to teach a student chef how ingredients work together than to give him a book of recipes, it is more valuable to help someone think like a professional services manager than to provide a cookbook approach to the professional services business.

Because the difference between *professional services* and *consulting* is becoming increasingly blurred, we will use the terms interchangeably throughout this book.

We'll start with the following service fundamentals:

- Professional services are not products
- Consulting organizations are different from product organizations
- People buy services in a different manner than products
- Selling services is different from selling products
- Professional services are different from other services
- There is a wide spectrum of types of professional services
- Companies must understand the competencies needed to win in the consulting game
- The challenges of a services organization in a product company are different from those faced by a consulting firm, such as KPMG or Deloitte & Touche

1

Think Services

*Professional services managers must learn
a new way of doing business.*

The name of the game in high tech has changed. Gone are the days of high product margins and soaring stock prices. Doubling the hardware speed every year is no longer the winning strategy. Companies are now looking for ways to differentiate their products and find new sources for additional revenue. One answer is professional services.

Product-centric companies can gain many benefits by expanding their offerings to include consulting services and integrated product-service solutions. Some of the ways companies can benefit include:

- A new revenue stream
- Pull-through revenues—product sales gained from the consulting relationship
- A way to differentiate the company's existing products
- More strategic customer relationships
- Enhanced account control
- Improved customer satisfaction
- Complete one-stop shopping solution for customers
- A chance for customers to focus on their core business while their vendor handles their specialized technology needs

Most product-centric companies fail to realize the vast differences between services and product organizations. Motivated by the benefits to products, customers, and the bottom line, they tend to underestimate the amount of time and resources required to launch a professional services business and stoutheartedly march ahead into the unknown land of services.

It's Not As Easy As It Looks

An established product company has a solid foundation—a company name, image, customer base, sales force, and operating infrastructure. With its product underpinning and proven success in building a business, entering the professional services business may appear to be relatively easy. The company can leverage its reputable name and image, and use its current sales force to sell to its current customers who have services needs related to their product needs. There are no new products to manufacture or ship. It appears the company only needs to promote the services and hire consultants to deliver them—then bill the customer and cash the checks.

Just as a couple adopting a baby has little way of assessing what challenges lie ahead for them—as well as for the baby—most product companies are unprepared for giving birth to a professional services business. From its product focus, it is difficult for the new parent company to foresee the challenges ahead.

Management in a product company sees the business world from a product perspective. They define their corporate strategies, select their target markets, identify customer needs, define the products they want to sell to these markets, manufacture the products, market them, sell them, ship them, and bill and collect revenue—all from a product viewpoint. The organizational structure, processes and procedures, sales compensation, and other business functions are designed to optimize operations of a product company.

Starting with a product perspective, corporations often fail to apply good business strategies and practices to services by either overlooking the need or using a product approach that just doesn't fit. For example, any good product manager knows that quality is important. Well-defined processes are created and managed in headquarters to control the quality of a product. Quality is as important, or perhaps even more important, in the services business. However, in the services business, services are sold before they are produced. How can service quality be controlled if the service is produced after the sale— and provided by individuals at customer locations throughout the world? As a result, the importance of service quality control is often neglected, or the knowledge of how to implement it is lacking when workers are dispersed and projects are customized.

To be successful, you must apply the fundamentals of good business to a professional services business: creating a business strategy, understanding your target markets, clearly positioning your services, promoting a brand image, hiring and retaining the best people, using effective sales channels, balancing supply and demand, ensuring quality services, providing an effective infrastructure, and meeting revenue and profit goals.

Yet, applying product thinking to the services business is not the answer. There are essential differences in the strategies and operations of product and services businesses. Professional services managers must learn a new way of doing business. You must understand the unique characteristics of services and services customers. You must see the world through the eyes of a services manager and services customers.

To help you make the transformation to a services viewpoint, we begin with a general description of services. Comparisons are drawn from an everyday life example to show you that you already know a great deal about buying professional services and that it differs significantly from buying products. *Looking at services through the eyes of a buyer* makes it easier to understand the principles needed to *sell* services. Once we have set forth the basic principles for buying and selling services, we will expand the services discussion to the high-tech world of professional services.

Services Are Not Products

Products are tangible. You can see one before you buy it. You can evaluate its physical characteristics. The seller can demonstrate the product's features and functions. Because most products are usually reproduced by machines, using highly refined and well-tested methods and quality-assurance processes, each one is an exact clone of the other.

You can methodically compare each of the features and functions of one product with those of another brand. Organizations such as Consumer Reports publish studies that compare and rank products based on extensive testing. In the technology world, trade magazines and websites publish studies that evaluate and compare competitive products.

Products have a price tag. Based on a comparison of features, functions, and price, you can reach a fairly objective conclusion about which product is most effective and the best value for your needs. You can do research to determine the least expensive place to purchase the product.

The risks associated with buying most products are fairly limited. If the product doesn't have all the features described in the literature and perform as stated, you can return the product. In many cases, the product includes a warranty and an extended warranty is available for purchase. If the product fails, you can have it fixed.

Services are intangible. You cannot see one or touch one. You can picture services that are simple and familiar, such as mowing the lawn. However, if the service is at all complex, it may be difficult to visualize and it cannot easily be demonstrated.

Services are provided by people—often ones you did not know before you purchased the service. The more complex the service, the harder it is for the service provider to standardize it into a reliable process and to train people to provide the same service consistently. In all cases, differences in personality and style of services personnel play a role in how the service is delivered and received. And the customer often plays an important role in the service performance.

You must buy the service before you can experience it. However, it is only after a service is experienced that you can measure the results. You may be able to get a refund or a discount if you can show that the service did not deliver what you bargained for. Or further work may be done to meet your requirements. Yet, how do you prove that a service has failed? You may have to resort to negotiation or litigation.

Getting a written specification or statement of work with detailed tasks and deliverables is certainly helpful. Yet, even with some remedy or remittance, you have at a minimum lost time in getting the results you desired. That time may result in lost opportunity. The service may meet the written agreement, and still may not meet all your expectations. And in some cases, such as a major systems integration project, poor results may result in millions of dollars of lost revenue or significant damage to a company's reputation.

Few complex services have set prices on a price list. A company is paid by the time and materials expended, or by a custom quote for the project. Even with a quote, you may not have anticipated everything that was needed upfront, and changes to the specifications may result in additional charges.

Buying Services versus Products

Given the invisible, elusive nature of services, it is no wonder that the prospect feels apprehensive making a purchase decision. Anticipated results—promised by the seller—are what people buy. They buy a promise. Understanding how people *buy* services is vital to knowing how to *market* and *sell* services.

Products: features, functions, price, and competition. For the purpose of comparison, let's start by looking at how people buy products. If you decide you want to purchase a personal computer, you think about how you are going to use it and what is needed to accomplish your objectives—how much memory do you need, how important is speed, what size monitor is desired. You decide how much you want to pay.

You may read product reviews in trade publications or on the Web. Once you see a product that meets your needs, you may look at competitive products in the same store, check out another store, or surf the Web. Your selection is based on features, functions, price, and competition. You also may be influenced by the reputation of a particular brand or its advertising, promotion, or product reviews. The more difficult it is for you to evaluate a product category, the more likely you will be influenced by the opinions of other people who are knowledgeable in this area.

Services: expertise, reputation, reliability, and trust. Next, consider how people buy professional services. Let's take the example of selecting the services of a doctor because that is something everyone can relate to. If you need a new doctor, how would you go about selecting one? You might start by seeking the services of a general practitioner to identify the general area of your problem. Or if you know the problem area, you may decide immediately to look for a specialist. For example, if you have a skin rash you would seek out a dermatologist. To select a doctor, people often start by asking their friends or relatives for referrals. During doctor visits, you develop an impression of the doctor's expertise from your interactions and the results. If you have a good experience, you continue to go to the same doctor—perhaps forever or until he retires.

So your initial selection is often based on a positive referral to a service provider who has the specific expertise you need. The ongoing relationship is based on your experience of the service provider's expertise and reliability, and the trust developed over time. The more serious your medical problem, the less likely that the doctor's fees are a major factor in your decision. In short, people buy services based on reputation, reliability, and trust. The more critical the service, the less likely price is an important factor. People evaluate services based on the expertise, reputation, and reliability of the service provider, as well as the personal interaction.

Selling Services versus Products

Next, let's look at how products and services are *sold*. As we examine the process using a simple example that everyone can relate to, consider how these same principles apply to the products and services in your company.

Product sales. Most product salespeople lead with their product. They present the features and functions of their product as well as its benefits. They may also explain why their product is superior to the competition. If price becomes an issue, the sales rep may be willing to discount the product or offer more favorable payment terms. This is consistent with the way people buy products—focusing on features, functions, price, and competition.

Services sales. Because people buy services differently than products, the product sales approach will not work for services. To discover a successful approach for *selling* services, let's study the step-by-step process for *how people buy services*. Consider our example of a person seeking the services of a doctor—let's call our services buyer Joe.

Identify pain. The process starts with Joe realizing he has a skin problem. If the rash is not irritating him initially, he may not be very motivated to see a doctor. However, if the rash spreads or is itchy, his discomfort will more likely motivate him to seek a solution.

So the starting point of a services or solution sale begins with the customer recognizing he has a problem or a situation he wants to change. Through effective questioning during the sales process, the service provider can assist the prospect in recognizing a problem or identifying areas for improvement.

Specialize. Joe seeks the services of a dermatologist, a specialist in the field of skin problems. He asks questions to select a specialist who has a great deal of experience in the particular field where he needs assistance. He may ask: How many other people have you treated with a similar problem? What treatment did you provide for other customers? What were the results?

The greater the level of experience and degree of specialization a service provider offers, the more likely customers will value the provider's services. Services marketing managers and salespeople must communicate effectively to their target markets the specialized expertise that their organization offers.

Provide referrals. To locate a doctor, Joe asks his family and friends for referrals. Joe's decision may be influenced by the level of enthusiasm references convey about their experiences with their doctor, the more closely their situation aligns with his own, and the number of referrals received for the same doctor.

Referrals or references play an important role in marketing and selling services. Because services are intangible and performed after the sale, customers seek references from people who have used an organization's services as a measure of quality and reliability.

Establish relationship. During the doctor visit, Joe mentally evaluates how well the doctor understands his problem and the doctor's prior experience solving similar problems. In addition, he assesses the doctor's interpersonal skills. Did he ask good questions? Did he educate me about my situation and my options? Was he a good listener? Did he show respect for my needs and opinions? Was he caring and understanding?

The ability to relate to a customer problem and establish rapport is a key success factor in selling professional services. This requires expertise in the subject matter as well as excellent relationship skills.

Competition is less important. If Joe respects the references, feels comfortable with the doctor's experience and expertise, and has a positive interaction with the doctor, he will most likely immediately decide to use the services of this doctor. The lower the level of trust or the more serious the problem, such as a critical heart problem, the more likely the person will seek a second or even third opinion.

Understanding and positioning your services vis-à-vis the competition is a factor in selling services, but usually not so large an influence as it is for products. The services of another service provider are normally only sought if the buyer becomes unhappy with the services he is receiving or if the service is complex or of a critical nature.

Price is less important. If the price seems reasonable, Joe will use the doctor's services without shopping around for the lowest price.

Generally, customers are not so sensitive to service prices as they are to product prices. As long as a service fee is not exceptionally out of line with customary fees, price is not a major decision factor. The more serious the problem, the less likely price becomes a deciding factor. Certainly, no one is seeking the lowest-priced brain surgeon. In fact, the reverse is usually true—higher-priced services are perceived as offering higher quality. Consulting organizations must price their services competitively, but in most cases low price is not a formula for long-term success. You may win an initial contract based on price, but if the service does not meet customer expectations, there will not be another engagement with that customer.

Customized service. Joe wants to understand his options, the pros and cons of alternative treatments, and the doctor's recommendation for the best solution to meet his needs.

Most problems have more than one solution. And most people want to be involved in the decision-making process. Product companies often place too much emphasis on packaging services into standard offerings. Although a packaged service assists the service provider to deliver a service, it is important not to lose sight of the value customers place on services that are customized to their needs—versus a one-size-fits-all approach.

Quality results. After receiving medical care, Joe evaluates the doctor on the effectiveness of treatment. Did the surgery, medication, or other treatment solve his problem? If the treatment was not expected to completely relieve symptoms or possibly even have created side effects, the doctor should have set appropriate expectations.

Customers who employ the services of a specialist expect to receive quality results in accordance with their expectations. Their level of satisfaction determines whether they continue to use the services of that specialist in the future. Setting clear expectations upfront, before the service work begins, is a key success factor.

Reliability. If Joe is consistently required to sit in the doctor's waiting room a long time before each visit, he may decide to find another doctor—unless the doctor was an outstanding expert and perceived as the only one who could provide the required treatment.

Just as customers expect products to be reliable, they also expect professionals to be dependable—not only during the sales process, but also throughout the services engagement. This means that consultants must meet all expectations as outlined in the statement of work as well as any oral commitments. Failing to follow through on promises can tarnish your reputation and can even result in legal action.

Trusted advisor. During and after treatment, Joe will evaluate his experience with the doctor based on both the results—how effective was the treatment, and the relationship—how comfortable does the patient feel with the doctor. If he has a good experience, he will continue to go to the same doctor—perhaps forever—or until the doctor does something that causes Joe to lose confidence in him. In addition, he will most likely recommend the doctor to his friends and relatives.

In a product sale, most of the work is complete with the sale; whereas in a services sale, the work is just beginning. In the consulting business, there is a saying, "you are only as good as your last project." The key to winning the next engagement is to ensure customer satisfaction in the current project.

Because everyone has hired and worked with medical professionals, and perhaps legal professionals, you already know what constitutes a good professional service and the factors that influence service provider selection and customer satisfaction. Spend some time thinking about professional services you have purchased in the past. How did you learn about alternative service providers? What factors played an important part in choosing the service provider you selected? Was price a major factor? Were you happy with the services you received? Did the quality of the services meet your expectations? Were the services completed in the timeframe promised? Was the service provider congenial? Would you hire this person/company again? Would you recommend the company to your friends?

Spending time reflecting on your service experiences will help you develop a services mentality, which will put you on your way to thinking like a services manager.

Professional Services Defined

Just as services are different from products, so are professional services different from other services. A *professional services organization* is any organization that uses the specialist knowledge of its personnel to deliver customized expert services. The remainder of this book is focused on professional services provided by high-tech companies. The basic principles are essentially the same as the ones described in our doctor analogy. Unfortunately, most managers in product companies who are new to professional services erroneously apply their product knowledge to the PS business instead of their experience interacting with doctors, lawyers, or other professional service providers.

There is a number of ways to define and segment professional services within a product company. Many companies include education services, and some include traditional support services—services designed to fix problems with the company's products. Education and support services organizations are often established early in the life of a high-tech product company. These service areas are more closely aligned with products and are usually better understood by product companies than consulting and implementation services. Sales, marketing, and operations for education and support differ significantly from consulting/implementation services. For these reasons, we will exclude education and support services from our definition of professional services.

Professional services offered by high-tech companies include the following:

- *IT Consulting.* Assisting managers and executives with decision making by providing professional assessment, analysis, and advice in one or more technology areas, such as business process reengineering, information technology (IT) strategies, architecture, implementation, and operations.

- *Applications Development.* Designing and developing new software applications or enhancing existing applications for customer business systems.

- *Implementation/Integration.* Assisting the customer in building an information technology infrastructure; and in implementing, testing, and deploying products, applications, and complete solutions.

  Integration services that result in a complete, operational system are classified as systems integration services. Platform integration services are a subset of systems integration services and do not include application development. They are often provided by computer hardware vendors.

- *Management/Operations.* Ongoing management or operations of an IT infrastructure. This includes services to improve the platform, such as system and network monitoring, performance optimization, and security services; services to manage the applications; help-desk services; and business-continuation services, such as disaster planning.

- *Business Consulting.* Services focused on providing business solutions for a company's business needs and problems.

- *IT Outsourcing/Facilities Management.* Whereas the prior services are provided on a contract basis according to a well-defined statement of work, IT outsourcing engagements are ongoing with contracts ranging from one year to ten years or more. In IT outsourcing, the service provider takes over responsibility for the ongoing management and operations of a complete IT facility or specific functional areas. This requires very specialized skills and management practices and is outside the scope of this book.

Although the term *IT consulting*, as it is defined by industry analysts, is limited to objective assessment, analysis, and advice to clients, it is often used more generally to refer to all professional services. So throughout this book, we will use the terms *professional services* and *consulting services* interchangeably. And we will refer to the organizations that purchase and use professional services as *customers*. Many professional services firms—including lawyers, accountants, and technology consulting firms—use the term *client* instead of customer. Some may argue that the term *client* more clearly accentuates the ongoing relationship with people who use the professional advice and expertise. However, for product-centric businesses, often the people or organizations that purchase the company's products and services are one and the same. So using one label provides consistency throughout the enterprise. Find out whether your company uses the term *client* or *customer* and be consistent.

Not All Services Are Created Equal

Not all professional services are equal. Marketing strategies and tactics will vary according to the type of service. The simpler the service, the more likely that marketing and sales tactics that work for products will be effective. Conversely, *the more complex the service, the less likely that product-oriented marketing and sales tactics will be effective.*

Simple services. Let's take the example of a service designed to install software for companies. For most software, this is a straightforward, routine task. The customer is simply looking for someone who can quickly perform this task in order to save the company time and resources. Low price and efficiency in performing the task are usually major deciding factors in choosing a service provider.

Product marketing and sales techniques are effective in selling a simple service. Marketing can describe the service in a data sheet, list it on a price sheet, or even package it into a standardized offering with a fixed price. A salesperson can easily describe the offering. And the consulting organization can easily define standard processes to perform a routine service and train consultants to deliver it.

Complex innovative services. In complex services, there is a high degree of customization and innovation needed to solve problems for individual customers. An example of a complex service is a large systems integration project, such as building a system to run a huge ecommerce business that must be continuously operational and support huge fluctuations in volume. Many complex services address enterprise-wide problems that solve important business issues. In highly complex services, the customer perceives greater risk in selecting a service provider. He is looking for "gray-haired" consultants who have a great deal of expertise in doing similar projects, ideally for customers in the same industry. Strong references are important; price is less of a factor.

Product marketing and product sales techniques will not work for complex services. Sales reps must use a consultative or *solution selling* approach (discussed in Chapter 9) to be successful. Marketing must focus on promoting the organization's reputation, quality, reliability, and expertise. An experienced project manager is required to manage the engagement. Consultants must customize the project for each customer. The work is performed at the customer site and usually requires a high degree of face-to-face interaction between the professional services engagement team and the customer team.

Instead of services merely being simple and complex, there is a continuum of professional services that vary from simple (can be performed with standard processes) to highly complex (require customized solutions for each customer and are delivered by consultants with a great deal of knowledge and experience). It is important to consider where each service falls on this spectrum so you can apply the most effective marketing, sales, and delivery techniques. Highly complex services that require a high level of customization, innovation, and ongoing interaction with the customer present some unique challenges in managing the service quality and the customer relationship.

Complex products. Complex *products* that are difficult for a customer to understand also do well with solution selling. For example, high-end servers or mainframes may be difficult for some customers to comprehend. The less the customer understands the product category, the more the sales team must build trust using references, expertise, and relationships. In addition, the customer's IT staff often needs assistance to implement a complex product. As a result, companies who sell complex products usually offer professional services as well.

In the next chapter, we will expand the service fundamentals to winning in the high-tech consulting services world.

Summary

There are essential differences between buying and selling products and buying and selling services. The simpler the service, the more likely that marketing and sales tactics that work for products will be effective. Conversely, the more complex the service, the less likely that product-oriented marketing and sales tactics will be effective.

2

Win the Consulting Game

Become a trusted advisor to your customers.

Customers hire professional services organizations to enable their company to solve problems or to gain a competitive advantage. Because a service is intangible and cannot be experienced or measured until it is delivered, customers must *trust* a professional services organization and individual consultants assigned to an engagement.

During the sales process, your sales team must demonstrate *expertise* to build trust. The customer expects you to clearly explain all the options, and recommend the best solution for his unique needs. During the engagement, the customer expects *quality* work delivered *reliably*—on time and on budget. The *relationship* that your account team builds with the customer during the sales process and engagement delivery is also critical to establishing trust.

The more positive experiences a customer has with an organization and every person within the group, the more trust is earned. Over time, the trust level can build to the point where the PS organization or specific consultants become a customer's trusted advisor. When a new opportunity arises, the customer may immediately seek the trusted group's advice and engage them even without considering any competing groups. On the other hand, negative experiences can result in a loss of trust to the point where a services organization may never again be allowed in the account. In fact, the customer may even stop buying the company's products.

In short, in order to win at the game of professional services, your PS organization must earn each customer's trust by demonstrating competence in the following areas:

Expertise: Have knowledge and experience in a specialized field

Quality: Accurately produce high-caliber deliverables

Reliability: Consistently meet all commitments as promised

Relationships: Show caring, individualized attention to customer needs

This chapter explores these sales and delivery success factors. Sales and delivery *processes* are covered in Chapters 9 and 11.

Expertise: A Ticket to Play

In order for your PS organization even to be considered for a consulting opportunity, you must select your core competencies, such as business continuity management or supply chain management, and develop expert knowledge and skills in the specialized fields.

As a PS organization in a product company with an established name, you have an advantage. Your company already has built a brand image in the marketplace. But even though your company is recognized for its products, your PS organization still needs to build its image as a provider of services and solutions in its core competencies, or areas of expertise. Marketing can assist in building your PS brand, but your consultants must participate in thought leadership programs and maintain a proven track record of demonstrated expertise in *all* engagements to reinforce the organization's image.

The positive image of your PS organization and its distinction as a specialist only buys you a ticket to meet with the prospect. The perceived expertise must be substantiated during the sales process. Demonstrating an understanding of the customer problem, presenting credible alternatives, and discussing experiences in solving similar problems for other customers all play a role in validating your organization's and your consultants' knowledge and experience.

Failing to establish credibility early on can quickly eliminate your company from consideration. I recall a time when I was working as a manager at a high-tech company, and we decided to consult with a market research firm about our professional services partner program. The decision boiled down to two market analyst firms. We held conference calls with both firms, but one company fully demonstrated a much greater understanding of the professional services business than the other firm.

When I contacted the losing firm, they pleaded for the opportunity to conduct another conference call. They claimed that they had people in the firm who were experts in professional services but had not participated in the first phone meeting. It was too late. We needed to move quickly, our impressions were formed, and a decision was made. First impressions count. Your company must bring in its experts who can establish credibility early in the game.

After an order is won, your consultants must demonstrate their expertise throughout the engagement. This includes properly setting priorities, anticipating problems, finding viable shortcuts, shifting gears easily, and applying expert project management techniques. Of course, no one can be expected to know all the answers. Consultants must not pretend to be an expert on topics when they are not. Instead, they must search out the answers or bring in other experts

Quality, Reliability, Relationships: How to Win

When a company receives a *product* order and ships the product to the customer, most of the work is done. In the *services* world, it is reversed—the real work begins when the customer decides to place an order. The services organization must finalize the statement of work for the contract, create a project plan, assign a project team, hire subcontractors, if needed—and then the major work of project delivery begins. Delivery must be marked by quality, reliability, and good relationships.

Quality. In order to win customer trust, your consultants must complete activities and deliverables in a first-rate way, in accordance with the written statement of work and any oral agreements. A good statement of work defines the scope of work, all requirements, schedules, and much more (covered in Chapter 9).

To consistently produce high-caliber work, consultants must have expert knowledge and be experienced at what they do. Less experienced consultants may need the help of more experienced specialists or well-defined processes. Achieving reliable, quality results during all engagements cannot be left to chance. PS organizations must invest in thoroughgoing training, delivery methods, and quality processes. Unfortunately, some new PS organizations, eager to become profitable, fail to make this investment and rely on individuals to instinctively produce well-crafted results for customers. It doesn't work.

In the product world, products are made in factories under quality procedures before shipment. But because the customer site (not the provider's factory) is the proving ground for services, it requires a greater sense of discipline to ensure that the project is performed smoothly and accurately the first time. Each phase and deliverable in an engagement contributes to the customer's perception of quality. And it is the customer's perception of whether the service is performed well that is the ultimate determinant of quality.

Reliability. Quality work is an absolute requirement for quality service—but not sufficient in itself. A quality project that is two months late may fail to accommodate the increased customer volume during the holiday season. A quality project that is way over budget will surely lose customer trust. Even chronic lateness for meetings or mishandling of invoices can significantly impact customer satisfaction.

Customers think of consultants as reliable and dependable when they can be trusted to do what they say they will do. This means meeting *all* expectations as outlined in the statement of work and any oral commitments. Reliability is important in project management, such as producing technical or business solutions on schedule and on budget, as well as in personal interactions like returning phone calls promptly or showing up for meetings on time.

In order to manage customer expectations, you must do a good job of setting clear expectations upfront about what is and what is not going to happen during the engagement. The statement of work should thoroughly establish all requirements and expectations, set boundaries on the project, and document any assumptions.

Once a statement of work is complete, you must document any deviances from it via change orders (a process used to make alterations to the original agreement). Lack of good change management procedures is a common cause of mismanaged expectations. If a customer makes a request that will greatly impact the committed delivery schedule and/or fees, failure to handle this upfront in a change request will affect your credibility with the customer.

When a professional services organization fails to deliver on promises made during the sales cycle, in the statement of work, during the engagement, or even following the engagement, it shakes customer confidence in the organization's capabilities and undermines its chances of building a reputation as a quality organization. A serious loss of credibility with a customer may be nearly impossible to recover from, and may also severely impact the company's image with other prospective customers.

Relationships. While goods are consumed, services are *experienced*. Customer satisfaction is heavily influenced by the personal interaction between the individuals in your consulting organization and the customer organization. Words, body language, eye contact, listening skills, and motives play a significant role. To some extent, a consulting team's relationship with the key contacts and the engagement team is often more important than the details of the technical solution. The customer may not be able to measure all aspects of the technical work, but he does know how he feels about your team's reliability, honesty, integrity, and dedication. He knows if he feels valued and respected.

It is up to your sales rep, engagement manager, and other people participating in a services sale to earn customer trust. Interpersonal skills play a key role. How well does your sales team listen to customer needs? Do they convincingly demonstrate expertise in discussions and presentations of potential solution approaches? Do they effectively communicate stories about similar experiences working with other customers? Does your sales team's body language, eye contact, and voice characteristics support and reinforce the credibility of verbal communications?

In most PS engagements, the account team is resident at the customer site interfacing with the customer team on a daily basis. This kind of visibility demands that your consultants be expert in their field *and* demonstrate good interpersonal skills. How they conduct themselves in the customer's presence—how well they listen, their level of empathy and interest in the customer's problem, their ability to persuade, how they handle disagreements, even how they dress—influence both the initial sale and repeat business.

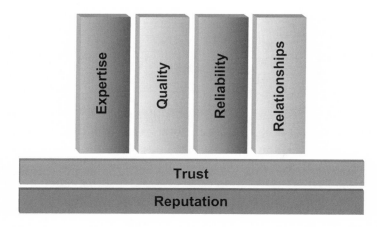

FIGURE 2.1   Four elements to win customer trust and build
        a solid reputation

Trust: The Reward

It is more difficult to earn trust in the services business than in the product business. On the other hand, trust in the services organization can lock in a customer forever. When a customer moves to another company, he will usually call on the PS organization he successfully used in his previous company.

PS organizations that:

- Demonstrate their knowledge and expertise in a specific service or solution area
- Produce high-quality work deliverables
- Prove their reliability and dependability
- Establish a positive relationship with the customer ...

... *earn substantial rewards—customer trust and confidence.*

In his book *The Marketing Imagination*, the late Theodore Levitt (economist and Harvard Business School professor) says, "The purpose of a business is to create and keep a customer. To do that, you have to do those things that will make people *want* to do business with you." This is certainly true for products—and it applies to professional services to an even greater extent.

FIGURE 2.2 Investment in solutions boosts competitive edge

A PS organization that invests in training, tools, methodology, knowledge bases, quality processes, and measurements to produce overall quality services and solutions also reaps the benefit of another reward—sustained competitive advantage. It is much easier for a competitor to copy a company's products, support offerings (maintenance and fix), and promotional campaigns, than it is for the competitor to try to reproduce all the elements that go into high-quality solutions. The PS organization can prove to be the company's most significant differentiator in selling services as well as products—just ask IBM.

Reputation: How to Play Again

Winning a customer's trust leads to more business with the same customer and referrals to new customers. With prosperous organizations, the cycle repeats itself again and again. Satisfied customers provide referrals—and those new satisfied customers provide more referrals. And that's how a PS organization builds a lasting solid reputation.

Reputation is greatly influenced by word-of-mouth communications. A company's marketing department can provide written customer testimonials and other promotional materials to influence reputation. However, no matter how great the work of the marketing department, a company's professional services reputation can only be as good as the engagements themselves.

The characteristics of professional services discussed in this chapter are true for consulting firms as well as professional services organizations in product-centric companies. However, launching and managing a PS business is significantly different for product companies than for consulting firms. In the next chapter, we will look at some of the differences.

Summary

To be successful, professional services organizations must:

- Have knowledge and experience in a specialized field
- Accurately produce high-caliber deliverables
- Consistently meet all commitments promised
- Show caring, individualized attention to customer needs
- Win the confidence of the customer
- Be recognized as trustworthy
- Earn and obtain customer references

3

Meet PS Challenges in a Product-Centric Environment

PS organizations must invest in quality processes and an infrastructure designed specifically for the services business.

Thinking like a services manager and understanding how people buy and sell services are important steps in building a professional services business in a product-centric company. However, a services mentality is only part of the success formula. In fact, you could be a highly successful services manager in a consulting firm and still fail as a professional services manager in a product-centric environment. You must understand the unique challenges faced in operating a professional services business within a product company.

On the surface, it would appear that attributes of a well-established product business—proven product leadership, a thriving sales force, a large customer base, and well-developed infrastructure—greatly simplify the job of building a services business. On the contrary, these factors actually contribute to some of the greatest challenges that a PS manager encounters. Understanding and effectively dealing with these factors can make the difference between success and failure.

Let's look at how a consulting firm is started and compare that to how a consulting organization is launched in a product corporation.

The Success Formula for Pure Consulting Firms

Typically, a consulting firm is started by one person or a few people who built expertise in a technical or business area while working for a successful company for many years. They decide to capitalize on their specialized knowledge in their field by starting their own business.

Their first customer is often their prior employer or one of their employer's customers with whom they worked in the past. If they do an excellent job for this customer, they get more business from the same company or referrals to other companies. Sometimes a client moves to another company and recommends them as a consultant. Other times a client refers them to their peers in the industry. In short, the business is built gradually, one customer at a time, with each success helping to win the next engagement.

The initial sales and marketing effort is usually provided by the consultants. Because the consultants have expertise and experience in their area of specialty, they can relate to the customer's pain, offer alternative solutions to the problem, recommend the best solution, and provide referrals from prior customers. Customers tend to trust the consultants and appreciate their straightforward, honest approach.

As the business grows, the consultants add resources and build infrastructure to support the consulting firm. They hire management who understand the consulting business. They hire salespeople who know how to sell consulting services. They design financial systems, legal services, and other departments from the ground up to support a consulting business. They create engagement processes, service methods, and training to support the development of consultants. All of the ducks are aligned and flying in the same direction—*all* resources and infrastructure are focused on services.

Without funding from a large corporation, a consulting firm is forced to grow slowly. The business is usually started with a focused area of expertise. The managing partners may add more solution areas and geographies as the business becomes more successful. If the firm gets off course in its early stages, it is usually small enough or growing slowly enough to make corrections easily.

In doing research on professional services firms, I called an owner of a systems integration firm with a long history of success in solving process and technology issues for top companies in the New Jersey/ New York area. They started with 2 people and grew to about 100 consultants over a 25-year period. They never experienced either the start-up or growth issues that are encountered by product companies moving into services. Like many successful consulting firms, they grew through word-of-mouth communications—each success helped generate another opportunity. During my conversation with one of the managing partners, I made some comments about how difficult it is for some people in product companies to sell services. The owner replied that he would not know how to begin to sell products; his entire experience was selling and delivering services. Selling services was second nature to him. He *thinks services.* As with most things in life, his perspective on how easy or difficult something is stems from his experience.

The Destiny of PS in Product-Centric Companies

In contrast to a standalone professional services firm, let's look at how a consulting business often gets started in a product company. A successful product company most likely has a large sales organization already in place, and has many customers who have purchased and continue to purchase their products. Some of these customers have expressed interest in services related to the company's products. As an initial step to meet its customers' services needs, the company may engage systems integrators or other consulting companies.

It starts with a good idea. The company later decides that it can sell more products by adding value from services, and, at the same time, produce additional revenues from selling services. Usually, support and education services organizations are established first.

Later, management makes the decision to start a professional services (consulting) organization. With a sales organization in place and established customers, building a successful consulting business looks like an easy task.

Initial PS staff is hired. The company hires a vice-president of professional services who then hires a small staff of legal, marketing, and finance personnel in headquarters. The new organization develops a few choice pieces of collateral to assist in the sales process, creates a standard contract for professional services engagements, and establishes a method to bill and collect fees. The new VP hires managers to launch PS practices in selected locations. Sometimes management moves support personnel into consultants' roles to bootstrap the organization. In other cases, they hire experienced consultants and technical people from management information systems (MIS) organizations or people with expertise in a business-specialty area.

PS' may lack the resources to support sales efforts. With a large sales force and a large customer base to draw from, initial customer opportunities usually come quickly—sometimes too quickly for a small, start-up organization. Sales reps looking for assistance on sales calls can't find a professional services person to join them on the call. Or they wait too late in the sales cycle to bring in a professional experienced in the services business. Other sales reps present opportunities to the PS organization and are turned away because there is no one to deliver the project in the timeframe needed or they are told that it is not the right type of project. The sales organization becomes annoyed that the consulting organization cannot entertain its requests. If these conditions continue, sales reps become disenchanted with the organization and stop promoting it to their customers.

Poor quality control impacts PS reputation. By hiring experienced consultants to launch the PS organization, some of the work will probably be top-notch. However, if consultants are given little training or direction or are asked to take on projects outside their areas of expertise, some consultants may miss the mark. Without quality controls in place, the law of averages tells us that sooner or later quality will slip.

When customers are unhappy, sales reps are unhappy. The word spreads faster through the sales organization than even the customer base. Soon the word is out—"the consultants do poor work, don't bring them into your account." "Their prices are too high." "Besides, they are never available when you need them to do a project. You can't even get them to go out on a sales call." And the situation spirals downward from there.

This scenario is oversimplified to make a point. However, many product companies that move into professional services end up playing out a similar scene. The sales force and professional services organization are not aligned. PS attempts to be all things to all people. Quality slips and customers are unhappy. And PS develops a bad reputation in the company. Now it has a more challenging problem— how to fix a bad reputation.

Why Product Companies Fail Where Consulting Firms Succeed

In the last chapter, we discussed the success factors of expertise, quality, reliability, relationships, and reputation. It all sounds so simple. However, if companies really were committed to these concepts, they would put processes in place to take on only those engagements that they have the expertise to deliver. This also means that every project would have to be delivered with high-quality results and careful response to customer needs.

Many of the problems that professional services organizations encounter stem from the following underlying issues:

- Lack of clarity on the PS mission
- Dynamics between the sales force and PS
- Inadequate investment in quality
- Inadequate investment in infrastructure

Professionals starting their own consulting firm rarely have these problems. There is no confusion about the business focus—because service is the only "product." Consultants either make their own sales calls or hire salespeople with skills and experience in selling services and solutions. The consulting firm invests in processes that ensure quality results—or they would be out of business without product revenue to sustain them. And as business grows, the firm creates an operational infrastructure that is designed specifically for a services organization.

Let's take a look at some of the potential problem areas that new professional services organizations in product companies face that typically are not encountered in consulting firms.

Lack of clarity on its fundamental purpose. A consulting firm is clearly focused on generating revenue from services, whereas the mission of some professional services organizations is to help drive product sales. The primary financial goal—product revenue *or* services revenue—is a key factor in how the organization will be managed and measured. Without clarity on its main purpose, PS can encounter significant problems in interfacing with the sales team and other organizations in the company. Decisions such as making consultants available to assist with product sales calls, discounting services, and investing in services that primarily propel product sales are difficult to make without clear-cut priorities. And the PS organization may be viewed as a failure simply because it is following one business model and being measured by another.

Dynamics between the sales force and PS. The relationship between the sales force and a start-up PS organization can be negatively impacted by the following situations:

- *Inexperienced sales team.* Product sales reps were hired because they are good at selling tangible products. Now the company is asking them to sell services and solutions. The less experienced the sales force is in selling services, the more assistance they will need from the PS team.

- *Sales/PS imbalance.* If a company has a large customer base with hundreds or thousands of salespeople and a small group of PS personnel to assist on sales calls, the PS folks simply cannot meet all the requests for sales support and the delivery needs, too.

- *Misaligned expectations.* Some sales reps may want to give away or significantly discount services to sell products and keep product customers happy. Whereas, a professional services organization that is expected to become profitable through its own devices needs to use its resources to earn revenue.

- *Poor communications.* Service promises are sometimes broken when communication isn't at the top of the list. Salespeople should not make commitments to customers before discussion of project feasibility. Services managers and consultants should be involved early in the sales process to assist in qualifying opportunities.

- *Poor business opportunities.* Salespeople who present inappropriate consulting opportunities to the PS organization may have their projects rejected. Even worse, some unsuitable engagements may be unwisely accepted and poorly performed.

When two people or organizations do not understand each other's perspectives, it's impossible to key into each other's strengths and objectives. The PS team blames the sales force for not bringing in good business or not bringing a services expert into the account soon enough. The sale organization may blame the PS staff for not stepping up to some proposed customer projects. Bad customer decisions are made, sales opportunities are improperly managed, resources could be squandered—and worst of all, consultants develop a bad reputation within the company and salespeople are even more reluctant to invite them into their accounts.

Inadequate investment in quality. With pressure to achieve profitability quickly, a professional services organization is usually eager to take on as much business as possible without investing in training and knowledge management programs. The more projects a PS organization takes on without proper skill development and engagement management processes, the more likely it will fall short of ensuring quality.

All of this pushes the organization to run before it can walk. Instead of just taking on the projects appropriate for the organization's level of experience, the temptation is to try and do whatever is needed to win product deals. A young organization needs to learn gradually from each engagement; develop experience; invest in service delivery methodology as well as engagement processes and procedures; and augment employee training to ensure quality results.

Expecting product infrastructure to support services. When starting a professional services organization in a product company, it may initially appear that the new organization can take advantage of the existing corporate infrastructure. In reality, a product infrastructure is not at all accommodating to a services business. Let's look at a few of the differences in the support functions for professional services versus products.

Finance. Financial systems in a product business are usually designed to process orders and invoice the customer when the product ships. The invoice may also trigger the payment of sales commissions. The systems used to process product orders, invoices, sales commissions, and other financial practices are not set up to handle services.

When an order for a service is placed, there is no product to ship. The customer is never invoiced upfront; invoices are sent on a monthly basis, or when major milestones are completed. Some engagements may last many months and salespeople do not want to wait for their commissions until the projects are completed.

The financial system must accommodate the unique requirements of a professional services business. Orders must be booked and customer purchase orders must be received before work starts. A time reporting system is needed to track the hours for each consultant and subcontractor for each project. Project expenses also must be tracked. Customers must be invoiced and subcontractors must be paid in accordance with the agreements. Unfortunately, product financial systems are not set up to handle these requirements. Trying to accommodate these issues with large, complex financial systems in product companies can be extremely taxing.

Legal. A product company usually has its own legal staff. This staff is skilled at creating legal agreements for hardware and software products, and support services. A professional services organization requires contracts and statements of work for customer engagements, contracts with partners, and agreements to hire subcontractors. The type of contract is different and the level of legal support is usually much greater than that required by product or support organizations.

Marketing. A marketing organization focused on products must change its mode of operations to achieve success in marketing professional services. Product marketing managers who take on this challenge typically face a steep learning curve. Support marketing managers are usually less prepared than product managers to make the transition. And services marketing managers from consulting firms must learn the ropes for operating within a product company. Ideally, a PS marketing manager with experience working in a product-centric company is the best fit. We will discuss PS marketing in detail in Chapter 7.

Methodology. Product companies have procedures to design, build, and manufacture products—and yet often fail to invest in an infrastructure to design and build services methodology. PS organizations need processes to manage engagements, and methods to leverage the reuse of marketing and delivery materials worldwide so consultants are not required to "reinvent the wheel" for similar services. The sooner the PS organization creates methods and tools that meet the unique needs of the business and shares these processes worldwide, the more efficient all professional services employees will become.

Amongst hardware and software companies in the IT industry today, IBM stands out as the one company that has grown its professional services organization beyond the toddler and teen-age stages into a mature, professional business. In fact, IBM Global Services is now the world's largest business and technology services provider. Since its early years in services, IBM invested heavily in its services infrastructure to ensure the quality of engagements. Other companies are stuck with a chicken-and-egg problem: they don't want to invest in a knowledge management framework and other processes until the organization is generating significant profits, and yet they can't grow their profits sufficiently until they make these investments.

Product companies understand that investment in R&D and production is required to be successful in the product business. But they often don't understand the process and infrastructure investment that is necessary to be successful in the professional services business. There are important lessons to be learned by looking at the factors that contributed to IBM's huge success in the services business.

IBM: The Premier Full-Service Provider

From the early 1990s, IBM was committed to becoming a world-class services company. In 1991, IBM restructured its Systems Services Division as the Integrated Systems Services Corporation, a wholly owned subsidiary dedicated to providing outsourcing services to customers. IBM's consulting organization was a subunit of its sales force. The organization focused on providing quality engagements that resulted in a high percentage of repeat business. In the initial years, it even overstaffed projects to build referenceable accounts and train inexperienced staff. Even though IBM's professional services business (excluding maintenance) was unprofitable until 1994, IBM stayed committed to its success.

In 1995, IBM unified its services business into IBM Global Services (IGS), lead by Dennie Welsh, to deliver seamless, integrated solutions to customers worldwide. Louis Gerstner (IBM's chairman and chief executive officer from April 1993 until March 2002) and Dennie Welsh had the foresight to see that the growing diversity in technology and products created the need for a general contractor to bring all the pieces together into a usable solution—integrating technology from various suppliers, as well as integrating technology into the processes of an enterprise. They envisioned IBM's becoming this general contractor for the IT industry

We can learn from IBM's experience by looking at some of the factors that contributed to its success in becoming the premier full-service provider in the IT industry. Most important, *IBM's top management team was committed to becoming successful in services. They were prepared to invest and to learn the business.*

Below, passages from Louis Gerstner's book *Who Says Elephants Can't Dance* attest to some of the challenges along the way.

IBM realized the importance of bringing together the product salespeople and services staff.

> Throughout those critical early days, it seemed there was a crisis a week between services and some other IBM unit. Many of our brand executives or sales leaders went ballistic every time the services unit proposed a product solution that incorporated a competitor's product. On more than one occasion I found one of these people in my office, railing against the renegades from services. My answer was always the same: "You need to invest the resources necessary to work with the services team to ensure they understand the competitive advantages of your products. View them as a distribution channel for your products. Your competitors do!"[1]

---

1.   Louis V. Gerstner, Jr, *Who Says Elephants Can't Dance?* (New York: Harper Business, 2002), p. 131. Reprinted with permission of Harper Collins Publishers.

IBM invested in people and the processes to support them. It unified its services investments worldwide to create one face to the customer and leverage its global intellectual property.

> Dennie ran just a United States services unit. There were dozens of other such services organizations spread all over the world. They had totally different processes, pricing, offerings, terms, and brand names. I asked Dennie to create a unified organization—still under the wing of the sales force—and introduce outsourcing and network services globally. This was a Herculean task—common problem solving, methodologies, nomenclatures, skill definitions, capturing and disseminating knowledge on a global basis, and hiring and training thousands of new people every year.[2]

IBM understood that the services business was different from the product business and that the company needed to invest years and capital to build the experience and discipline it takes to succeed.

> I will state unequivocally that services businesses are much more difficult to manage. The skills required in managing services processes are very different from those that drive successful product companies. We had no experience building a labor-based business inside an asset-intensive company. We were expert at managing factories and developing technologies. We understood cost of goods and inventory turns and manufacturing. But a human-intensive services business is entirely different. In services you don't make a product and then sell it. You sell a capability. You sell knowledge. You create it at the same time you deliver it. The business model is different. The economics are entirely different.[3]

---

2.   Ibid. pp. 131-132.
3.   Ibid. pp. 132-133.

A key factor in IBM's success in the services business is its commitment to superior customer service. A central theme of Lou Gerstner's book is how he reorganized the company around a commitment to customer service. He saw the marketplace as the driving force behind everything at IBM. Listening to customers and providing customer satisfaction became one of the company's central values. This cultural change provided the foundation to build a successful services business—and lead the company in a spectacular turnaround.

Because IBM has successfully made the transition from a technology-led hardware company to a services-led model, the challenges outlined in this book, for the most part, no longer apply to IBM. They think services. They get it!

Summary

In product-centric environments, PS must align itself with the mission, goals, and strategies of the company. It must determine how to utilize the talents of a marketing team and sales force skilled in marketing and selling products to advance services. And it must get funding and support to build quality processes and an infrastructure that serves the needs of a services business—not a product business. IBM is a role model of a high-tech company that faced these challenges and successfully worked through them.

PART II

The Building Blocks of a Professional Services Organization

In Part I of this book, you learned to change your orientation from a product to a services perspective.

In Part II, we will look at services strategies to launch and manage a professional services business, and operational practices to market, sell, productize, and deliver services—as well as manage partner relationships.

Building Blocks of PS Business

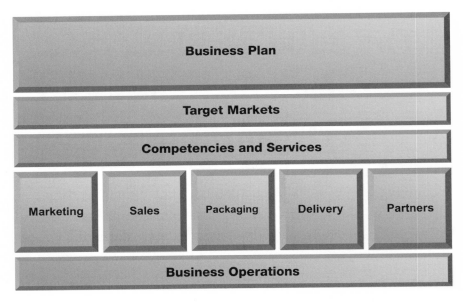

In the diagram above, the building blocks of a professional services organization look very similar to those of a product business—because fundamentals of good business management apply to both product and services businesses. The differences lie in the content and execution of the strategies and operational practices—as you will discover in Part II of this book.

4

Build Plans and Strategic Alignment

*The **primary** goal of your professional services organization should be definitive—to generate services revenue OR to increase product sales.*

At the heart of any successful business is a robust business plan. A professional services business is no exception. Whether you are a manager starting a new professional services business or taking over the management of an existing PS organization within the company, you need to define the mission and goals of the organization and ensure that the company's executive team understands and buys into the organization's strategic direction.

This chapter covers the following topics:

- Issues to consider when developing a PS business plan
- PS organizational structure
- Creating alignment within the PS organization

Create a Business Plan

My intention here is not to teach you how to write a business plan—there are plenty of books and articles about that—but to share a few key points about business plans that are important to keep in mind when starting a professional services business. The first point is simply that *you need a business plan*.

A business plan serves as your roadmap to success. It defines where you want your business to be and how you plan to get there. It becomes the framework to build and operate your business. And it provides a benchmark against which your organization's performance can be measured and reviewed. To keep your business plan current, conduct an annual review.

A good place to start is with a short strategic plan (2-4 pages) that articulates your organization's mission, goals, strategies, and objectives. The mission defines the fundamental purpose of your organization or simply why your organization exists. It helps create a work environment where there is a common purpose. The goals state what you want to accomplish through the business. Clearly, your goals must be aligned with your mission or you will be going in different directions at the same time. Strategies describe actions or activities designed to achieve your goals. And objectives state what is going to be achieved and when it will be achieved, converting your goals into specific performance targets.

Stated very simply:

Mission = *overall purpose*

Goals = *what* is to be achieved

Strategies = *how* to achieve goals

Objectives = *measurable targets (what and when)*

Your short strategic plan becomes the foundation on which to build a more comprehensive business plan. Once your short plan is approved, you can expand it to define your target markets, core competencies and services, organizational structure, growth plans, and profitability goals. A complete business plan includes strategies and goals for marketing, sales, service delivery, partner relationships, and financial management (see Table 4.1). You can present the plan in a formal, detailed document or a simple presentation. There is no single acceptable format.

Some guidelines to keep in mind when creating your plan follow:

- Participate in your company's mission and goals
- Establish your fundamental purpose
- Get buy-in from all stakeholders
- Align financial goals with your mission
- Build a system to monitor and measure success

Let's take a closer look at each of these points.

Participate in Your Company's Mission and Goals

When you launch a new professional services organization in a product-centric company, you aren't stepping into virgin territory—the company has been doing business for some time. The PS organization must align itself with the company's mission, goals, strategies, values, markets, and products. It's the best winning game plan.

A standalone consulting firm doesn't have the same considerations. Its total focus is on its services business. As stated by educator and lecturer David Maister in his book *Managing the Professional Service Firm,* most professional services firms aspire to:

- Deliver outstanding customer service
- Provide fulfilling careers and professional satisfaction for its people
- Achieve financial success so that the firm can reward itself and grow [4]

Most professional services organizations in product companies strive to achieve these goals and more, as outlined in Table 4.2. Many of the goals listed in the table relate to the company's products and the product customer base—creating alignment between the professional services organization and the larger product-centric corporation.

---

4.   David H. Maister, *Managing the Professional Service Firm,* New York, NY: The Free Press, 1993, p. 3.

TABLE 4.1 Components of a PS business plan

- Summary
- PS mission/goals/strategies/objectives
- Core competencies and services
- Target markets
- Sales and marketing strategies
- Delivery strategies
- Partner strategies
- Management and organizational structure
- Financial management

Being part of an established corporation has many advantages. To capitalize on your company's strengths, do a SWOT (strengths, weaknesses, opportunities, threats) analysis for your company and your PS organization. It will aid you in taking an objective look at your business so you are better prepared to make important decisions about your competencies, markets, partner strategy and other strategic areas. Discover the company's strengths that can help open doors to opportunities for your PS business. Find areas where services can open new markets for your products. If relationship selling is a company strength—or a weakness—you must consider that when developing your PS sales strategy. Do the company's threats single out areas you need to avoid—or areas that professional services can neutralize and even build into strengths? Seeing the big picture, you can create synergies and avoid potential minefields.

Establish Your Fundamental Purpose and Get Buy-In

A mission statement is not a long list of goals. It is a singular statement and defines your fundamental purpose—why you are in business. It is designed to share internally what the organization was formed to do and should not be confused with a positioning statement (described

TABLE 4.2 Professional services organizational goals

- Deliver outstanding customer service
- Generate services revenue
- Add value to products
- Create a competitive advantage
- Increase sales of products
- Offer total solutions
- Increase credibility with customers
- Improve account control
- Reach new markets
- Provide one-stop shopping

in Chapter 7), which is externally focused and communicates how you wish to be perceived by your target markets.

It is not uncommon for a professional services organization to have multiple goals, such as the ones listed in Table 4.2. Showing how many ways PS can add value to your company may help justify your existence. However, you must avoid ambiguity about the primary revenue role that professional services plays in your company. Otherwise, you could be setting the stage for unsolvable dilemmas and even endless bickering between professional services and other organizations in the company. In other words, you must plainly answer the question:

Is the *primary* revenue goal of your professional services organization to generate services revenue *OR* to increase product sales?

To answer this question, it is imperative that you involve your company's executives. And in addition, sales managers, product managers, and other stakeholders must understand your mission, embrace it, and commit to support it. Issue resolution and requests for funding should go smoothly if you have buy-in upfront on your organization's mission from all appropriate parties.

With clarity, for instance, you'll be able to easily answer the following questions:

- Should PS personnel invest a great deal of time assisting on sales calls?
- Should presale support be treated as downtime when calculating utilization rates (described in Chapter 14)?
- Should a service be deeply discounted to help sell a product?
- If a service is discounted or delivered free, should the sales organization compensate PS?
- Should PS invest in creating a packaged service to support the introduction of a strategic new product if the service in and of itself will not generate significant revenue?

Achieving clarity on your mission will significantly improve your relationships with product sales, product marketing, and other groups. And it will provide a basis for setting goals and strategies for the PS organization.

Vendor neutrality. Your mission will influence your position regarding vendor neutrality. If your mission is to increase product sales, you are likely to recommend your company's products to meet sales goals. Whereas, if your mission is to become a services-lead company and generate services revenue, you are more likely to provide an unbiased analysis of all available product offerings and recommend the one that best suits the customer's environment and needs. You need to weigh your obligation to help the customer select the best products—even if it is a competitive product, versus your loyalty to your own company.

IBM Global Services presents itself as vendor-neutral: selecting the best hardware and software to meet the customer's needs—regardless of vendor. Vendor neutrality or vendor preference can raise issues from two perspectives. First, if the services organization does recommend competitors' products, it may create animosity with the product organization. Second, the customer might wonder if a services organization in a product company can really provide objective product recommendations. At the same time, it is important for companies that offer comprehensive solutions to appear to be vendor neutral. Whatever your position regarding recommending competitive products, your consultants must understand and honor it.

Other strategic topics. Clarity on the mission also sets the stage to resolve other strategic issues such as the following:

Add-on services or total solutions: Are professional services tactically positioned as an add-on to your products or strategically positioned as an integral part of a combined product-service solution? The answer will influence how you structure your sales model.

Product- or services-led sales: Do professional services lead or follow the product sale? For example, a service to install and configure a product would *follow* the product sale and be sold as an add-on to the product, whereas a data protection solution to reduce the risk of data loss or data corruption might *lead* the sale and pull through product sales.

There is no right or wrong approach. You simply must determine the best strategy for your business. Establish and communicate your mission—and other strategic issues—when you launch your PS business and continually review it as the business evolves. As a new business, it is likely that your fundamental purpose is to drive product sales, and your sales strategy is to lead sales with products and sell services as an add-on to products. As your business matures, your mission and strategies will evolve too. For example, you may decide to focus on selling product-service solutions that address specific business problems. As your priorities change, be sure to communicate the new strategies to all stakeholders and get their buy-in.

Align Financial Goals with Your Mission

Establishing your mission and prioritizing your goals set the ground rules so that operational and financial goals, objectives, and measurements can be aligned accordingly. Getting executive buy-in to your strategic direction, or mission, is also essential before moving ahead. An organization that fails to do either may end up being viewed in a negative light simply because its revenues and profits are being measured against the wrong business model. For example, if your PS mission is to drive product sales, achieving break-even status may be all that is expected. However, if your mission is to generate a new source of revenue from services, obviously more is expected. And if your goal is to become a services-led business, the PS organization needs to reach an even higher level of profitability.

Set realistic financial goals. Once you have established your mission and key strategies, you are ready to build a financial business model.

- Estimate your start-up expenses and your operating expenses
- Establish the utilization, revenue, profit, and gross margin goals for PS
- Determine the percentage of profits that will be allocated to sales, marketing, intellectual property management, consultant training and development, contract development, finance management, and other expenses

Obtaining financial results from other companies for comparison can be challenging because the quarterly and annual financial results for most IT companies combine support services, education services, and consulting services under the broader umbrella of "services." In general, the margins for consulting services are lower than reported for all services because higher margins for support services skew the results.

By looking at the gross margins for competitors, you can get a general idea of what to expect. For example, IBM's gross profit margin for services in 2007 was 28 percent compared to a total gross profit margin of 42 percent for the company. IBM clearly has a mature services business with more than half its revenues generated from services. And yet, its services margins are lower than what many companies expect from their services business. So be sure your financial goals are aligned with your services strategy, and are realistic for your industry and your organization's level of maturity. Thomas E. Lah provides good information on setting financial goals in his book *Mastering Professional Services.*[5]

Allow time to become profitable. Frequently, a product company starts a professional services organization with the belief that it will quickly expand its profits from this business. A company needs to set realistic expectations and understand that it will take a year or two for a new organization to reach its profit goals. During the first few years, a human-capital-intensive business needs to hire consultants and train them, establish a customer base, and build an operational infrastructure. It is most important that the team is building referenceable customers—the profits will come later.

Monitor and Measure Success

There is an old management adage: You can't manage what you don't measure. Typically, companies rely on financial measurements to gauge an organization's success. However, these measures reflect past performance and often generate a short-term reactive response. Other measures are needed to help align business activities to the organization's mission, goals, and strategies, and encourage a long-term strategic response.

To meet the need for a more a comprehensive view of a business, Robert Kaplan and David Norton developed a performance management tool called the Balanced Scorecard and published the concepts in the Harvard Business Review in 1992 and their book *The Balanced Scorecard.*[6] The Balanced Scorecard has evolved into one

5.   Thomas E. Lah, *Mastering Professional Services*, Westerville, Ohio: Professional Services Press, 2005.

6.   Robert S. Kaplan and David P. Norton, *The Balanced Scorecard: Translating Strategy into Action*, Harvard Business School Press, 1996.

of the world's leading methodologies for measuring organizational performance and achieving exceptional and sustainable results.

Following are the Balanced Scorecard's four different perspectives on organizational performance and a short description of how they apply to professional services (see Table 4.3 for sample PS measures):

Customer perspective. Customer measurements indicate how well professional services are delivered to the customer. Customer satisfaction is a leading indicator of success for all businesses—especially professional services. If customers are not happy, they will not request future engagements and may generate negative word-of-mouth communications.

Internal process perspective. Internal process measures focus on the activities and key processes required to deliver the value expected by the customer. One key measure is the time between the promised completion date and the actual completion of an engagement.

Learning and innovation perspective. Learning and innovation measures focus on the skills and capabilities that are required to support customer engagements, as well as measures of innovation (such as new approaches, competencies, or technologies).

Financial. Focuses on the traditional financial measurements used by most any organization (revenue, expenses, profit, gross margin) as well as measures specific to professional services (utilization).

The Balanced Scorecard measures are *balanced* in several ways:

- Between *external measures* for shareholders and customers, and *internal measures* of critical business processes, innovation, and learning and growth
- Between the outcome measures—the results from *past efforts*—and the measures that drive *future performance*
- Between *objective* and *subjective* measures

TABLE 4.3 The Balanced Scorecard: Sample measures for a
PS organization
(For each measure, define your objective, target performance goal, and key programs required to achieve your objective.)

Customer	Internal Process	Learning	Financial
• Customer satisfaction • Market share • Customer retention • Customer referrals • Customer success stories • Service quality rating	• Quality control • Partner program management • Risk management • Employee productivity • Project completion on schedule	• Skill development • Employee turnover rate • New competencies • New technologies	• Backlog • Service revenue • Pass-thru revenue • Operating expenses • Profit per engagement • Gross margin • Utilization rate

Entire books, detailed Web-based papers, and consulting firms are available to guide you step-by-step in implementing a Balanced Scorecard. My objective here is simply to point out the need for meaningful performance measures (metrics) that will align your operations with your strategies and keep your team committed to continuous process improvement. The Balanced Scorecard is a proven and respected methodology for monitoring success.

Corporate Resources: An Aid or a Hindrance?

In addition to defining your mission, goals, strategies, and measurements, it is also critical to align your PS organization with other departments in the enterprise.

A new professional services organization in a product company is handed a two-edged sword. On the positive side, it has:

- A clear source of funding
- Other functional units to call on—legal, finance, marketing, and MIS

- Image and reputation of the parent company
- Built-in product customers with some degree of loyalty to the company
- Usually a dedicated direct sales force with established customer relationships

On the other hand, building a services organization in an established product company presents its own set of challenges. And like many situations in life, some of the assets also present the challenges. As a member of the PS organization, you would like to look to the resources in the product or support organizations to help you. However, these professionals have their own primary company obligations and may be too busy to respond to your requests, and most likely want your support.

In fact, the number of requests from large product organizations can easily overwhelm the scarce resources in a start-up PS organization—especially because services organizations usually run a tight ship to keep their non-billable employee overhead down. As a marketing manager in the PS organization of large product-centric corporations, my first priority was the needs of my own PS organization. However, I often was frustrated by the amount of my time that was consumed working with product and support marketing organizations. Because these organizations were much larger than our start-up PS group, meeting their needs often stretched our sparse resources. For example, an upcoming company product launch included many planning meetings and ate into our time. The larger marketing organizations could afford to have one of their marketing personnel participate in the numerous meetings. But it was a drain on our precious PS marketing resources to attend these meetings when very little time was spent on issues that related to our services. On the other hand if we didn't participate, our messages were often misrepresented or not included.

To successfully work with product organizations, you have to educate personnel on the unique nature of the services business. And that requires a good deal of time and patience. Frequently, product companies establish professional services organizations in order to provide their customers with total solutions. But product marketing managers, who don't understand professional services, may simply lump consulting services with technical support services. Services are relegated to one slide at the end of a product presentation—rather being presented as an integral component of the solution. You need to relentlessly pursue educating your peers about the nature, value, and role of professional services in solutions.

Establishing a solid relationship and clear communications with sales, marketing, finance, and other supporting personnel throughout the company is crucial to the success of your PS business.

PS Organizational Structure

In addition to managing relationships outside your PS organization, you must master the intricacies of working within your own organization. As a project-oriented business, most PS organizations use a practice model to bring together the right mix of talent to sell and deliver services successfully and profitability.

What is a practice? A professional services practice is a group responsible for part of a services business related to a particular market. In high-tech companies, practices are typically organized in the following ways:

Geographic practices. The geographic practice is responsible for selling and delivering services within a designated geographical area. The size of the area varies by the size of the organization and the amount of potential business in an area. For example, a PS organization may devote one geographic practice solely to New York City and another to all of the South Eastern United States. Geographic practices are a practical way of organizing to reduce travel costs and deploy employees who understand the local market, customs, and language.

Competency or service line practices. A competency or service line practice is aligned with the service offerings provided to a particular market. For example, a Business Continuity Management practice may offer comprehensive services to meet customer needs in this area, including contingency planning, business resiliency, and disaster recovery.

Industry practices. Professional services organizations that deliver business consulting services may have practices aligned by industries, such as banking, financial markets, health care, and telecommunications.

Matrix model. Many professional services organizations have practices that combine geographic practices and competency practices or geographic practices and industry practices. Typically, the consultants reside in—and report directly to a manager within—a geographic practice (such as the Chicago practice or the Paris practice). The manager is responsible for their career planning and wellbeing. At the same time, consultants belong to a competency practice (such as the Storage Practice or the Java Practice) that focuses on developing their skills in the specific competency. This provides the best balance of practice management (e.g., minimizes travel, provides proficiency in the local language) with the ability to cultivate and leverage strong competency skills. Consulting engagements may be staffed with a mixture of specialists from geographic, competency, and industry practices.

PS roles in a practice. A professional services practice typically has a relatively flat organizational structure. The key roles include:

Practice manager. The practice manager or director has overall responsibility for the practice, including the delivery team and sometimes the sales team. The role encompasses managing business plans and budgets, as well as forecasting demand and hiring, leading, and mentoring the teams. Practice managers also assist in making sales calls and closing business deals.

Engagement manager. Engagement managers play an instrumental role in the development and management of projects and client relationships. During the sales cycle, engagement managers participate in sales calls, proposal and SOW development, and forecasting. During the delivery phase, engagement managers may provide oversight and guidance to project managers or manage a team of project managers on large projects.

Project manager. Project managers develop project plans (scope, activities, schedule, cost), and manage the consulting team and the implementation of projects to ensure that projects are delivered on time and within budget. To be most effective, project managers need a base level of knowledge about the content of the engagements.

Consultants. Consultants deliver the services in accordance with the agreements defined in the statements of work. In most cases, consultants work at the customer's site. In a high-tech company, a consultant is typically a technical role, but basic project management skills are also important.

Business development manager (BDM). Business development managers assist the sales team in identifying and qualifying new business leads for professional services, and help drive sales opportunities to closure.

Entrepreneur or Franchise Operation?

One of the most challenging alignment issues that the PS organization faces is within its own walls. What is valued—centralized leadership from headquarters or autonomy and entrepreneurship among individual outlying offices? Is your organization a franchise or a loosely held federation?

Products are inherently centralized. Because most products are produced in a centralized controlled environment, companies can easily ensure the consistency of their products worldwide. Headquarters determines distribution channels, sets prices, defines permissible discounts, creates brochures and data sheets, and provides support centers. Designated production facilities build the products. Sales offices worldwide typically sell the same products—with minor differences to accommodate local preferences. The interpersonal dynamics and cultures may vary from office to office, but the products usually remain the same.

Intangibles breed decentralization. While most products are not easy to customize, the intangible nature of services makes it feasible for each PS office to define its own set of service offerings, set its own prices, and create its own marketing collateral. Not only can services be changed, it is desirable to adapt them to best meet each customer's specific needs. Because labor prices vary around the world, there is also justification for variation in hourly rates or service prices. Consulting firms value autonomy. By the nature of the services business, it is less likely—and less desirable—that each office be a cookie-cutter copy of another as in a franchise operation. Given the high degree of professional judgment needed to be responsive to unique customer needs, consulting organizations require managers who can "think outside of the box" and address the numerous decisions that must be made on a regular basis.

A highly decentralized model has drawbacks. While there are clear benefits for professional services organizations to operate autonomously, there are also many drawbacks. As we discussed earlier, alignment with your company's mission and goals is important. Likewise, to operate efficiently, practices must benefit from each other's strengths. From an internal perspective, companies suffer financially by duplicating staffs and process development at every level in the company. By standardizing marketing materials, sales and delivery training, methodology, and business processes, companies benefit from economies of scale. A highly decentralized model also encourages turf battles among the various geographies.

At the same time, customers come to expect a certain amount of standardization from multinational corporations. The products are the same, so customers foresee being able to get the same services in all locations with a consistent level of quality. Multinational customers who are looking to purchase similar products and services for multiple offices worldwide may be frustrated by companies who lack consistent services and global standards for quality.

Collaboration has payback. Product companies value centralization. Consulting firms value autonomy. There are pros and cons to each model. So how does a professional services organization in a product-centric company position itself? You must find a balance that respects the needs and culture of your corporation, and also provides the flexibility and local autonomy that best suits the nature of your consulting work.

It is critical that the vice president of professional services establish a collaborative environment so the organization can take advantage of the collective power of all the practices. At the same time, it is important that the leader make decisions and take a stance on which issues and practices must be standardized worldwide.

Some of the ways to create synergy among the practices include:

- Encourage practice manager to share ideas for running the business
- Establish a compensation plan to reward a practice to provide resources to another practice
- Encourage consultants to share knowledge and experience learned during engagements
- Create a mechanism to allow individuals to work on methodologies that contribute to the overall organization
- Recognize and reward people who contribute to the overall success of the organization

Summary

The first step in launching a professional services organization is building a solid business plan. Be sure your plan contains clear goals that are aligned with the corporate mission and product goals, and is understood by all key stakeholders in your company. Determine whether the fundamental purpose of your PS organization is to increase product sales or be a singular, major revenue source.

Professional services organizations must strike the right balance between operating as a franchise with a consistent business image and operations, and providing the flexibility for each office to address the unique needs of its local markets. Failure to do so can result in loss of economies of scale or inability to meet unique customer expectations.

Questions for Consideration

What are your PS organization's strategic objectives?

Whether your PS organization is large or small, new or well established, you must ensure that you have a well-defined business plan that has been endorsed by your executive team and other key stakeholders. You must also build successful alliances with the product organization, and strike the right balance of power within your own walls. Here are some questions that will help you get to the heart of your strategic objectives.

- Does your PS organization have a business plan?
    - Are the mission and goals well defined?
    - Have you identified the target markets for your services?
    - Do you have well-defined strategies for marketing, selling, and delivering your services?
    - Do you have an effective partner strategy?
    - Does your company's executive team support the plan?

- How are professional services positioned in relation to your products?
    - Is the fundamental purpose of your organization to increase product sales or generate revenue from services?
    - Are services strategically positioned as an integral part of a total product-service solution?
    - Are services positioned to lead or to follow product sales?

- Are your services aligned with the company's business strategy?
    - Are your services positioned as independent of your products so that you can recommend a competitive product, if it offers the best solution?

- If your services are designed to support your company's major products, do you recommend competitive products that play a less strategic role in the total solution?

- Does your PS organization have well-defined financial goals?
  - Are the financial goals well aligned with your services mission?
  - Are your financial goals realistically achievable?
  - Is professional services a profit center or a cost center?

- How is your PS organization structured?
  - Are practices organized by geographies, competencies, or industries?
  - Do your engagement managers manage projects, manage other project managers, or assist in selling services?
  - Do you have business development managers to identify, qualify, and help close sales opportunities?

- What is the relationship of your headquarters organization to other groups in the company?
  - Do your company's executives understand and value the PS business?
  - Do other managers and supporting professionals—marketing, sales, finance, and legal personnel—understand services and the role it plays in the company?
  - Who makes the decisions about what services areas to focus on—your consulting practices or your product organization?

- How do your geographical consulting practices interrelate?
  - Is your organization a franchise or a loosely held federation?
  - How are decisions made in your organization?
  - What is the role of your headquarters organization versus the local consulting practices?
  - How are knowledge and experience shared within the organization?

5

Target Your Markets

Producing quality results that create referenceable customers in your targets markets—that is the key to long-term success.

A new professional services organization in an established product company is ripe for over-commitment. Here's why. Being part of an established product company with a solid image and reputation can initially make it easy for a new PS team to obtain many engagements. There is a readily available customer base and a sales force that has built relationships with these customers. And PS management is often eager to sell services, generate revenue, and become recognized in the company. So in order to reel in the most business, PS may cast a broad net, offering a wide range of services related to the company's entire product line.

The larger the product line, the more services—and skill sets—are needed. Confronted with the immensity of opportunity presented by a large established product customer base, PS organizations can lose focus, chasing every opportunity that presents itself—like a "junk yard dog," gobbling up whatever someone throws over the fence. The result: Over-commitment.

But getting the opportunity for services engagements is only half the battle. To achieve success, you must produce quality results and build referenceable customers. To accomplish this in a consistent manner, you must define your core competencies, markets, and services; and take a market-driven approach to sales. Before we discuss these steps to success, let's first take a closer look at the risks of taking a sales-driven approach to services.

Relationship Jeopardy: Consequences of a Sales-Driven Approach

The goal of a sales-driven company is to maximize sales and sales revenue. Pressured to meet quarterly goals, the sales team may be willing to do anything and everything to get orders and make the numbers. Using the sales-driven approach, the sales team focuses on pitching the vendor's products versus understanding the customer's problems. This only succeeds in producing short-term results.

When selling professional services, salespeople are unlikely to make a sale without understanding the customer's problem. Yet, there is even a greater danger than not making a sale. In its eagerness to be successful, a new professional services organization may take on projects for which its consultants do not yet have the skills to deliver in a quality manner. If the organization spreads its resources too thin before it is has built expertise and quality procedures, it may end up one day in an engagement where, no matter what it does, the consultants cannot meet the customer's expectations. The goal then becomes how to get out of the situation without being sued, having the engagement show up as front-page news, or being used as fodder for competitive organizations to feed to customers. Bottom line: The consequences of being sales driven—especially during the early years of an organization—can be fatal. The PS organization's reputation may be damaged in the eyes of the sales organization and worse— perhaps in the marketplace.

After being burned by a few failures, PS usually learns the importance of thoroughly qualifying engagements. Over time, it becomes more selective about the projects it takes on and it begins building quality control procedures.

For Success: A Market-Driven Approach

A market-driven company focuses on building a loyal customer base. Instead of simply pitching its products and services to any customer to make a sale, a market-driven company strives to:

- Focus on specific markets
- Understand the problems of its markets
- Build customer relationships
- Deliver high-quality solutions
- Demonstrate reliability
- Win customer confidence and respect
- Develop a reputation as a trusted advisor

Commitment to superior customer service was a key factor in the success of Lou Gerstner's strategy that led IBM to become a world-class services company in the mid-1990s. He saw the marketplace as the driving force behind everything at IBM. Listening to customers and providing customer satisfaction became one of the company's central values.

A Market Defined

In *Crossing the Chasm*, Geoffrey Moore—lecturer, author, and consultant on marketing and sales strategies—defines a *market* as:

- A set of actual or potential customers
- For a given set of products or services
- Who have a common set of needs or wants, and
- Who reference each other when making a buying decision[7]

This definition of a market applies as much to professional services markets as it does to product markets. Let's look at the best way to apply the definition.

---

7. Geoffrey A. Moore, *Crossing the Chasm , Marketing and Selling High-Tech Products to Mainstream Customers* (revised edition), HarperCollins Publishers, New York, 1999, p. 28.

Customers, actual or potential. When you are starting a services business in a product-centric company, the best companies to target are the ones currently using your products or technologies. Once you have built a PS business, your established services customer base provides real potential for new engagements. Of course, to keep your business thriving new customers must continually be added.

Customers who have a common set of needs or wants. Before analyzing customer wants and needs, identify and prioritize your core competencies (described in Chapter 6). Select ones that align with your company's mission, business strategies, and products. Then identify customer wants and needs—both technical and business— that relate to your core competencies.

Consider the following questions:

- What *technical* challenges do customers *need* to solve? (e.g., mitigate security threats, data loss, poor performance)

- What *technical* goals do customers *want* to achieve? (e.g., gain benefits from the latest technology)

- What *business* challenges do customers *need* to solve? (e.g., process an increasing volume of orders)

- What *business* goals do customers *want* to achieve (e.g., increase revenue, reduce expenses, speed time to market)

Customers for a given set of services. Consider your core competencies when defining service offerings that provide solutions to your customers' wants and needs. Some services may relate to one core competency, and some may take advantage of your expertise and skills in multiple areas. When services are customized and innovative, it may take "broad brush strokes" to paint an overall picture of your offerings.

Customers who reference each other when making a buying decision. Establishing a strong word-of-mouth reputation with your customer base is absolutely essential for successful marketing of high-tech professional services. To accomplish this you must target customers who reference each other. And, of course, you must deliver high-quality services on time and within budget to ensure each reference is a positive one.

When defining your markets, you need to consider all of these customer characteristics. For example, a company that sells business process management (BPM) products may define a target market as large financial companies in the United States that need assistance in implementing the vendor's products. Another company that sells supply chain management (SCM) products may target large manufacturing companies that are current product customers, and want assistance developing effective processes to control the operations of their supply chain. Still another company that sells storage products may target small businesses that need help with protecting heir data. Don't assume that your market needs to be huge. Selecting well-defined markets that you can serve effectively is a better approach.

Crossing the Chasm—for Services

In *Crossing the Chasm*, Moore advocates that a company focus on a single market, a beachhead, and use it as a springboard to adjacent markets in order to cross the chasm (moving the product from early adopter acceptance to early majority acceptance). His recommendation pertains to high-tech products, but market focus also applies to building a customer base for a service line.

In the professional services business, you can cross the chasm—move a service line from a few customers to wider marketplace acceptance—by following these steps:

- Focus on a specific market
- Deliver an engagement with quality results
- Create a referenceable customer
- Repeat the above steps with a new customer in the same market

By focusing on specific markets and competencies, your organization can build expertise in well-defined areas. Specialized expertise leads to quality results. And high quality serves as one of the key principles underpinning the professional services business. A PS organization must ensure that customers are extremely pleased with all aspects of services engagements in order to create a customer base that will provide good references. By targeting customers in the same market who reference each other, word-of-mouth promotion will help pave the way to your next sale.

The future of a professional services organization is dependent upon its reputation and references. When starting a new organization, it is more important to produce referenceable accounts than it is to drive revenues. If a customer is positive about the overall *quality* of work, the *reliability* of the consultants, and the personal *relationship*, more business with the same customer and referrals to new customers will follow.

In *Crossing the Chasm*, Moore talks about the importance of ensuring that customers who are critical in establishing a strong word-of-mouth reputation get not just the product but what he calls "the whole product—the complete set of products and services needed to achieve the desired result. Whenever anything is left out from the set, the solution is incomplete, the selling process unfulfilled, and the customer unavailable for referencing."[8] In like manner, PS customers must be pleased with "the whole service"—not only the quality of the consultants' work, but also the consultants' soft skills such as communications and other interpersonal skills, and project management skills such as keeping commitments, adapting to change, and meeting deadlines. By ensuring that customers are extremely pleased with all aspects of the services engagement, you can create good referenceable accounts that can provide the basis for future wins in the selected market.

---

8.   Geoffrey A. Moore, *Crossing the Chasm , Marketing and Selling High-Tech Products to Mainstream Customers* (revised edition), HarperCollins Publishers, New York, 1999, p. 68

With prosperous organizations, the cycle repeats itself again and again. By delivering engagements with quality results, you generate positive word-of-mouth communications and references. You can leverage the references in one market to win customers in adjacent markets. For example, manufacturing customers may not spread the word to finance customers. However, you can take your story about how you reduced storage costs for a manufacturing company and tell it to a banking company who has a similar storage problem. Many high-tech solutions work equally well across industries, making it easy to leverage your successes across horizontal markets.

Over time, you can add additional service lines and repeat the process. Customer by customer, market by market, is how a professional services organization gradually builds a lasting solid reputation.

Specialization: Key to Quality Control

Just as a product company starts out by specializing in one product, adds more products to the product line over time, and gradually builds additional product lines, so must your services organization. Imagine how disastrous it would be if a new product company decided to build many different high-tech products simultaneously and tried to sell them to diverse markets. Specialization allows your PS team to build solid expertise in specific areas and deliver services that require this expertise to well-defined markets.

By putting all the wood behind one arrow, you can align your resources to achieve quality results. PS managers, consultants, marketing, and sales can team to identify markets, define market strategies, and bring together all the elements to ensure success, including:

- Understanding wants and needs of the market
- Optimal services and solutions for the market
- Defining skill sets needed to deliver these services and solutions

- Consultants who have the skills to deliver these services
- Additional training necessary to ensure quality delivery
- Understanding competitors and their strategies
- Training salespeople to identify the target market, converse with customers about their wants and needs, and describe how your services can address these needs
- Strategic partners (if needed) for sales and delivery
- Database that can be used for lead generation
- Promotional materials, sales guides, and presentations to support the sales efforts
- Customer satisfaction requirements

By focusing on solutions for a specific market, your organization's expertise builds with each sales call and each engagement. Consultants obtain customer input, deliver services, refine the service materials, deliver the refined services, get more customer input, and continue to build expertise in an iterative process. Based on your successes, the PS organization can create methodology and tools to make it easier and faster to deliver your solutions to additional customers with even higher quality results. If appropriate, they can create packaged services for the market. Managers can better identify additional people to hire with the specialized skills needed to complement your existing staff. In the meantime, marketing managers can work closely with engagement managers to use the new intelligence to refine the service positioning and messaging.

Over time, you can add more competency areas and target new markets as the resources of your organization grow. By focusing on a few key areas at a time, you can gradually build a professional services organization with services in all the core competencies to support your company's business strategies and complement your company's product line. The lessons you learn from one market can be applied to build additional core competencies and solutions targeted to new markets.

Summary

Demonstrating expertise and establishing showcase accounts in a specialized area are key factors in selling more services to the same market. The test of success is the customer's ongoing satisfaction, leading to an eagerness to give references. Securing these much-needed references requires focus on core competencies in target markets where you can deliver quality results on time and within budget.

Questions for Consideration

Who are your target markets?

Professional services organizations cannot be all things to all people. You need to focus on target markets. Here are some questions for consideration to help your PS organization build referenceable customers in target markets.

- Does your company use a sales-driven or market-driven approach to selling professional services?
  - o Are you focused on specific markets? Or do you take the "junk yard dog" approach and accept any projects that come your way?

- Who are your target markets?
  - o Do you have referenceable customers in each market who are willing to support your marketing and sales efforts to other customers in the same market?
  - o Do you have documented customer success stories for each target market?

- Is your organization prepared to sell and deliver quality services to your target markets?
  - o Do you have marketing materials to assist in selling services to each target market?
  - o Are your salespeople trained to sell the appropriate services to your target markets?
  - o Do your consultants have the skills and experience required to deliver quality services to your target markets?

6

Create Your Services Portfolio

Developing and sustaining specific competencies
are essential to achieve your business goals.

To lay the groundwork for a successful professional services business, you must have answers to these questions:

- What are your core competencies?
- What markets do you target?
- What services do you offer?
- How do you select these services?
- How do you gather feedback to enhance your services?

We will address these questions in this chapter.

Define Your Core Competencies

Core competencies are areas of specialized expertise that provide competitive advantage, deliver fundamental customer benefits, and can be leveraged across multiple markets. They reflect what an organization does best. In high-tech PS organizations this proficiency commonly takes the form of knowledge, skills, and experience in a particular technology area, such as storage management or network architecture. A core competency could also relate to the ability to integrate multiple technologies, or a unique methodology that provides sustainable differentiation, such as the McKinsey method used for problem solving. Some high-tech PS organizations, such as IBM and Hewlett-Packard, also have core competencies in business solutions and industries. See Table 6.1 for examples of core competencies.

PS must *align its core competencies with the company's business strategies to help achieve the company's mission.* Mission is *"what"* a company wants to accomplish, and strategy is *"how"* the company will achieve it.

To select core competencies that are aligned with your company's strategies, you need to take a close look at your company's customers, products, markets, and competitors. A SWOT analysis—looking at your company's strengths, weaknesses, opportunities, and threats—is also valuable. Based on this information, it becomes possible to define the sorts of competencies you must develop and sustain in order to help your company achieve its goals.

For each core competency considered, assess whether it is too narrow or too broad to align with your company's business strategies. For example, if one of your company's strategies is to develop data backup and restore products targeting the Fortune 1000 market, then storage management may be too broad a core competency for your PS business. In this case, data protection may be more appropriate.

If you select multiple core competencies, prioritize them so you can focus on building expertise in one or two areas at a time. By limiting the focus and playing to your strengths, your consultants can build the skills necessary to deliver high-quality services efficiently. However, this does not imply that core competencies are static; as your business evolves, your core competencies also need to adapt and change.

Create Strategies to Reach Your Markets

After you define your core competencies, you can select your markets. As described in Chapter 5, a market is a set of customers, with a common set of needs or wants, for a given set of services, and who reference each other when making a purchase decision.

What markets will you target? Following are some factors to consider when identifying your target markets:

- *Company size.* Small, medium, or large enterprises
- *Current or new customers.* Current product customers, current services customers, or new markets
- *Current or higher-level managers.* People your sales team calls on today or higher-level executives who can help your company be viewed as a more strategic player
- *Vertical or horizontal markets.* Companies within a specific industry or markets across industries that share a need
- *Geographic locations.* Companies within specific states or countries; or geographies that share a common language

Do research to ensure you understand the wants and needs of your target markets for your core competencies. Talk to analysts. Read industry or technical journals. Attend technology conferences. Conduct focus groups or surveys. And most important—talk to customers in your target markets.

How will you reach your target markets? For your core competencies, assess the demand for services in each market and the competition's ability to offer the volume and quality of services to meet the demand. You may be able to move into an established market by offering higher-quality services or a more innovative approach. Also consider the following factors:

- *Custom or packaged offering.* Will your consultants customize your service offerings for each customer? Or will you offer packaged services?
- *Marketing.* What marketing programs and tools are needed to sell your services?

- *Sales resources.* Can you use your existing sales force to sell your services? Will you need to hire new sales reps, create a new sales force, or train your existing sales team? Do you need to create alliances with partners to sell your services?
- *Pricing.* How will you price your services? Time and materials? Fixed-price quote? Value-add pricing?

These topics will be covered in subsequent chapters of this book.

Identify Your Services Offerings

Just as a product organization develops a product roadmap, you need a roadmap that outlines the services that you plan to offer—services that align with your core competencies and address the needs of your target markets.

Following are some of the questions to address when defining your services:

- *Customer needs and wants.* What are the wants and needs of your target market that relate to your core competencies? Which of these will your services address?
- *Benefits.* What business results will your customers experience from your services?
- *Competition.* What consulting firms or professional services organizations offer comparable services? How will you differentiate your offerings?
- *Product alignment.* How closely will your services be aligned with your company's products?
- *Portfolio compatibility.* How will a new competency align with other competencies in your portfolio?
- *Expertise level.* What level of expertise is required to deliver the services? Does it match the expertise level of your consulting staff?

TABLE 6.1 Sample core competencies

Technologies

- Application development
- Application integration
- Application management
- Asset management
- Business continuity and recovery
- Capacity planning
- Desktops
- Facilities management
- Middleware
- Networks
- Performance
- Platform integration

- Security
- Servers
- Service-oriented architecture (SOA)
- Site and facility
- Software development
- Storage
- Strategy and architecture
- Systems integration
- Systems management
- IT consolidation
- Wireless technology

Business Consulting

- Business intelligence
- Business process management (BPM)
- Customer relationship management (CRM)
- Enterprise resource management (ERM)
- Enterprise resource planning (ERP)

- e-Commerce or e-Business
- Financial management
- Human capital management
- Knowledge management (KM)
- Portal solutions
- Supply chain management (SCM)
- Wireless e-commerce solutions

Industry Expertise

- Banking
- Consumer products
- Education
- Electronics
- Financial markets

- Government
- Healthcare
- Insurance
- Retail
- Telecommunications

As discussed earlier, your core competencies define the breadth of your expertise. In the health-care profession, dentistry is an example of a core competency. However, a dentist may decide to limit the breadth of his core competency to a specific dental subfield such as periodontics or endodontics. After choosing to narrow his specialty or core competency to periodontics, the dentist may decide to limit his services to treating gum recession and providing dental implants. Of course, once he identifies his services offerings, he must ensure that he has all the skills to deliver the services in a quality manner, or find a way to acquire the skills.

Likewise, an IT professional services organization must first select its core competencies with the appropriate breadth, and then determine the depth of services to offer within each core competency. For example, a PS organization may select storage backup and recovery as its core competency, and then decide to offer services both to assess the customer's current environment and to design and implement backup and recovery solutions. In the future, the company may decide to add services to analyze storage and network capacity requirements for backup operations or services to optimize backup performance. Just as competencies are not static, services offerings within each competency must continue to evolve as the PS organization matures.

Ensure Service Readiness

After identifying a *product* for a target market, product companies know that there is still a great deal of work required before the product is ready to launch. Good principles of product marketing and development are followed: market analysis, product requirements definition, quality assurance tests, alpha tests, beta tests, and limited release. Initial product production is scheduled to meet market projections. Sales and support organizations are trained on the new product. When all departments associated with the product are ready—including quality assurance, manufacturing, operations, channels, customer support, marketing and sales—the product is launched.

Let's contrast this process with what often happens in the services world. A list of services is identified to complement the company's product offerings. Management hires consultants to deliver the services and announces the availability of the services or solutions to the sales organization. End of story.

The same companies that put a great deal of effort into understanding product marketing requirements and ensuring quality products often fail to put the same level of effort into defining services marketing requirements and ensuring services are delivered in a quality manner. Clearly, both product organizations and services organizations must define the target markets, identify strategies to reach these markets, and ensure that processes are in place to produce quality results.

The point here is that you can't simply hire consultants and hope for the best. Just as a product company does its best to ensure product quality and reduce costs, PS needs to provide strategies, processes, and infrastructure to ensure the quality of its services.

Before announcing a new service or service line, consider the following:

- *Marketing.* What programs or sales tools are needed to sell the services?
- *Sales.* Does your sales team need to be trained?
- *Delivery resources.*
    - What skills are needed to deliver your services?
    - Do you have the resources with the skills to deliver the services?
    - Do you have enough consultants who can deliver the services in order to meet the anticipated demand?
    - Will you need to hire or train consultants to deliver the services?
    - Will you require subcontractors to deliver your services?
    - Will your services prompt systems integrators to hire your consultants to assist in the deployment of large-scale solutions?

- *Delivery tools.* Are methodologies, questionnaires, or tools needed to effectively deliver the services?

- *Measurement.* How will you measure customer satisfaction? Do you have a formal mechanism in place to gather input to improve your services?

Aligning with Your Company's Key Products

Your company has an image in the market. Your products align with your company image and meet the needs of your target markets. When you are starting a services business, the best place to begin is with markets that are aligned with your products and services that add value to your products.

Take the path of least resistance. Your product company's relationship with its market opens the door for you to sell services to the same market. Your company has built strong ties with your customers. The sales team and management have visibility into the services your customers need. You can call on those customers to better understand their needs; and help you define, test, and refine service offerings. Your PS team has credibility simply by being part of the product company.

Services that add value to products can jumpstart a customer's product experience. With these services, customers can develop a solution plan, install and configure the product, optimize the use of the product, or educate their staff on best practices for using the product. These introductory services can open the door for follow-on consulting engagements.

By focusing on services that add value to your products, your product and sales organizations will likely be supportive. Be sure to tout your successes to your sales team so they appreciate the fact that your PS organization helped customers get the most value from your company's products in the shortest period of time.

If you are launching a new PS business, consider starting with a core competency and services that align with your company's *most important product or technology*—the one that is most closely associated with your corporate identity. When I was a marketing manager at Sun Professional Services, Java technology was an obvious choice. When I met people outside the industry, they would ask me if I still worked for that Java company. In some cases, they could not remember the name of the company or even knew what Java was, but it was closely associated with the company. When the services opportunity was related to Java, Sun easily won the business. The Java specialists developed more expertise with each engagement and could call on Java product specialists in headquarters for advice if needed. It was easy to position the company against the competition in this area and win the business. After all, who wouldn't want to receive Java assistance from the company who invented it?

Consequences of aiming too high for your market—and your competencies. Instead of starting with services aligned with your products, some PS organizations aim higher in order to help the company reach executives and be viewed as a more strategic player. A company that too quickly attempts to offer high-end strategic services outside the scope of its products may encounter several obstacles:

- Lack the skills to deliver the services
- Be unable to attract or retain the appropriate consultants
- Lack sufficient credibility or sales skills to reach the appropriate stakeholders
- Be perceived by the sales force as competition instead of as an integral part of the product solution

Several years ago I worked with a customer who sells security products. During its early years in the professional services business, the company hoped to establish itself as a leader in business continuity management services in order to be perceived as a more strategic player in the security market and reach more top executives.

At the time, the company fell short of achieving its goals. It initially attracted senior consultants in the European practices, but lacked the structure to transfer the skills to other geographies and eventually was unsuccessful in retaining the talent in Europe. The company needed to gain more expertise, references, and credibility in delivering services more closely tied to its security products before taking on more strategic service areas, such as business continuity.

To be successful, product-centric companies should first master the art of professional services by delivering services that provide value add to their company's products before attempting to make the leap to higher-value services that address more strategic business goals in new markets.

Offering Total Solutions

Another successful approach is to provide a total solution, including hardware, software, and services. This solution may be targeted to a specific vertical market or may be applicable to a wide range of industries.

Depending upon the product line and the breadth of skills in the services organization, it may not be feasible for your company to provide the total solution alone. You may need to connect with systems integrators and/or product companies to provide parts of the solution while identifying specific roles for your own products and services.

When I was at Sun, there was a group of sales representatives dedicated to selling hardware for Enterprise Resource Planning (ERP) solutions. This group teamed with companies that provided the ERP software—SAP, Baan, PeopleSoft, and Oracle. However, in many cases, the customer first hired the systems integrator who selected the hardware and software vendors. The integrator knew how to improve the business processes and integrate the business applications, but frequently lacked the skills needed to integrate specific hardware and operating system platforms.

ERP systems integrators were more inclined to recommend a vendor who could provide the platform integration services without competing with them in the systems integration space. Because Sun fit these criteria, a solution of Sun hardware and software combined with systems integrator ERP services and Sun platform integration services was one that was likely to be sold by the ERP systems integrators as well as by the Sun sales team.

The marketing and salespeople responsible for ERP at Sun requested that the Sun Professional Services organization provide the Sun platform integration services for ERP solutions. Seeing this as a niche market without high rewards, the PS organization was initially reluctant to invest in this area. Sun's ERP organization clinched the deal by offering to invest in these new services. Sun PS started a new ERP practice and hired a practice director, a marketing manager, engagement managers who had expertise in ERP, and a few ERP technical experts. In ERP consulting engagements, the ERP specialists were supplemented by technical consultants from the local geography practice with general skills in platform integration. This well defined market solution was extremely successful in generating significant product and services revenue. Opportunities continued to grow while the marketplace for ERP expanded.

ISVs that provide software related to customer relationship management (CRM), enterprise application integration (EAI), business intelligence, and other business solutions can identify similar solutions that combine their software and services with the broader skills of systems integrators.

Providing a total solution requires teamwork among product marketing, services marketing, sales, professional services, and partners.

- Marketing materials—brochures, service briefs, sales guides, presentations, white papers, success stories—must be specifically targeted to the whole solution

- Sales representatives should be taught to present the complete solution offering
- Systems integrators selling the solution must have a clear understanding of your company's value-add
- Engagement managers must be hired with expertise in the competency or trained on the specific solution

Services-led solutions typically result in pull-through sales of products and additional services—a big win for your company. And your customers gain the advantage of one-stop-shopping and an integrated solution that has been proven at other companies.

Partnering with Systems Integrators

In many ways, implementing a software application is like building a house—the project is dependent on a wide range of talents to be successful. Like the builder who needs experts to prepare the land, connect to public utilities, and perform a wide range of other specialized activities, the software implementer must build a new information technology infrastructure or connect to an existing infrastructure, and project manage all aspects of the effort.

Many product-centric companies—at least in the early stage of their consulting business, and perhaps forever—have to rely on systems integrators to provide many of the specialized talents. Systems integrators assist customers in building an information technology infrastructure, as well as in the implementation, testing, and deployment of applications. Although an integrator may subcontract many aspects of a consulting project, it is still responsible for delivering the overall solution on time and on budget.

Because systems integration projects require both in-depth project management skills and breadth in a wide range of areas, it is advisable for a new PS organization to gain experience in more specialized areas and smaller projects before undertaking large systems integration engagements. Whereas, by providing consultants to team with systems integrators, product companies can gain incremental revenue, form stronger ties with their product customers, and strengthen their relationships with systems integrators who can recommend their products to other customers. New consultants can also learn on the job by participating in engagements managed by experienced systems integrators.

Bottom-up Approach to Service Selection

In most product companies, the managers in the corporate organization make the strategic decisions about markets and products that become the focus for the business. In many cases, the company's customer advocacy and product marketing organizations work together to obtain information directly from customers in order to enhance or design products. This way of working certainly makes a great deal of sense for products. Because this is the way the corporation operates, many solutions and services are also selected in this manner. However, this top-down approach is not effective for choosing services.

While the factory for products is in headquarters, professional services are created and delivered by consultants at the customer site. Consultants spend each day living with customers, hearing about their needs, and implementing solutions. Practice managers, engagement managers, and salespeople who are involved in selling professional services are knowledgeable about customer needs. Marketing managers must make the time to get out in the field and talk to these sources to ensure that the focus for new services is on the appropriate solution areas. This approach becomes particularly important when selecting best services for packaged solutions.

Because consultants have the unique opportunity to live with customers, they also provide a source of input to product managers. They can share valuable information about customers' product experiences to refine both the products and the sales approach.

Input That Improves Your Services

PS managers and marketing managers can obtain ideas for services improvements or new services through debriefings with customers after the completion of an engagement, individual meetings between professional services managers and key customers, periodic meetings with groups of customers, or customer surveys.

Engagement debriefings. At the end of every engagement, the practice manager or engagement manager should meet with the customer to obtain feedback on the engagement: what went well, what went wrong, and what areas need improvement. With real project details, you can make process improvements and apply lessons learned to new engagements. The debriefings are not about blame. Everyone should feel free to speak openly without fear of repercussions. This meeting may also provide information that could lead to additional projects with the same customer.

Key customer visits. Practice managers, marketing managers, and other professional services players can also learn a great deal by meeting with individual customers periodically. These meetings could be held at the customer's office or over dinner. They can enhance the customer relationship as well as provide a way to gather input on how to improve the service delivery, or become informed about opportunities for new services.

On these visits, it's always more important to listen than to speak. Accurate listening is based on the desire to understand. A good listener knows why he is listening, looks at the speaker, shares responsibility with the speaker, determines the speaker's purpose, and remembers important points.

User groups. User groups are another effective means to gather customer input. For each key practice, ask a small group of customers to attend periodic meetings to discuss service offerings. You can gain feedback on how to improve current offerings, obtain input on plans for services, and gather ideas for additional services. This is also a good way to enhance customer relationships.

Customer surveys and analysis. To gain a more in-depth perspective, conduct a formal study of your top customers. Build a profile of your customer base by analyzing the industries that the customers represent, which customers provide repeat business, the percentage of total revenue per customer, the geographical locations of customers, and the types of services delivered. Survey your customers to learn what criteria they use to select a professional services organization, why they selected your group, what they consider your strengths and weaknesses, and what factors distinguish your team from the competition. This information will help improve your image as well as your services.

Increase Customer Trust and Loyalty

In addition to gathering input from customers through meetings, surveys, and other means, PS organizations can create a mutual dialogue and partnership with customers through customer advocacy and executive sponsor programs.

Customer advocacy program. A good customer advocacy program focuses on aiding customers to improve productivity, reduce operational costs, and become successful in many other ways. With customer advocacy programs, powerful links are built between the customer and your company. Customer satisfaction increases and positive word-of-mouth enters the marketplace. The results are great customer references that translate to increased PS sales. A customer advocacy program also provides a way for you to learn more about the performance of your business partners. Most product-centric companies already have a customer advocacy program for their products. This program can be extended to include professional services.

Executive sponsors for key accounts. Another way to increase customer satisfaction and loyalty is through an executive sponsor program. Assign a highly experienced senior manager to each of your top accounts and ask them to meet with these customers at least twice a year. In this way, your top customers have an advocate and a sponsor throughout the relationship lifecycle. Your company may already have executive sponsors for product accounts who can take on the responsibilities for professional services relationships.

Summary

Do research to select the best markets for your services and understand your customers' requirements. Demonstrate expertise, quality, and reliability in services engagements to establish showcase accounts. Securing good references builds a strong reputation and leads to more sales in the same market. Over time, you can add new competencies to address the needs of additional markets as your organization's experience and resources grow.

Start with services that provide value-add to your products before making the leap into strategic services to new markets. This approach is most likely to win the support of your product sales force, product marketing, and the existing product customer base. Over time, you can build additional competencies and move to more strategic solutions if that is part of your overall services strategy.

Questions for Consideration

What are your competencies and services?

Here are some questions for consideration to help you create or improve your services portfolio.

- How do you select your core competencies, target markets, and service offerings?

- Are you investing in the services that align with your company's key products and the solutions most needed by your customers?

- Do your service offerings:
    o Provide value to your company's products?
    o Assist customers with technologies related to your products?
    o Address strategic business goals in new markets?
    o Integrate hardware, software, and services?
    o Complement systems integrators' offerings?
    o Meet unique requirements of vertical markets?
    o Provide innovative solutions?
    o Employ your organization's unique methodology?

- Who is providing the input needed to select the highest value target markets for PS and the appropriate services for these markets?
    o Are practice managers, engagement managers, and consultants involved in the selection process?
    o What processes are in place to obtain customer input?

- How do you obtain customer input to improve your services?
    o Do you meet with the customer to obtain input at the end of each engagement?

- o   Do you periodically visit with key customers?
- o   Do you conduct user groups or customer surveys?

- Does your PS organization participate in your company's customer advocacy program? Or the executive sponsor program?

7

Adapt Marketing to Services

*Professional services marketing
is different from product marketing.*

To ensure your company's success in selling services, you must select your target markets and understand their primary needs. You must decide what services you will offer, what your unique positioning is, who your competitors are, and what your most effective promotional tactics are. You must establish a brand image. In short, you need a marketing department.

Services marketing is different from product marketing. Marketing managers who understand the unique aspects of marketing professional services within a product-centric company are essential to your success.

Organizational Dynamics

All product companies have a marketing organization—or at least one person—that possesses a wide variety of marketing skills vital to the success of the business. Product marketing managers focus on understanding customer requirements and interfacing with the software development or engineering organization to ensure that quality products are built to meet customer needs. Marketing communications managers focus on messaging, positioning, collateral, and outbound programs to describe and promote the company and its products. Web managers, public relations, and advertising people offer their special skills. All of these people understand products and the company's processes for launching and promoting products.

When professional services are added to a company's offerings, a number of decisions must be made to determine where PS marketing fits in the company.

- Do you create a marketing department dedicated to professional services, or can PS be managed by the product marketing department as just another product line?
- If you create a PS marketing department, does it report to corporate marketing, product marketing, services marketing, or directly into the PS organization?
- Should PS marketing staff be added to remote practices, or only reside in corporate?

Let's take a closer look at these options and the best approaches for the PS business.

Marketing staff experience. Don't expect that the product marketing team will market your services. It is important to have marketing personnel dedicated to professional services. And, because PS marketing is different from product marketing, it is best to hire marketing professionals who have experience in *professional services marketing* with other product-centric companies. A services marketing manager with experience at a large consulting firm is a good second choice, but she must learn the unique aspects of services marketing in a product company. A product marketing manager with experience in your company is another possibility. He knows your company, its products, and the product marketing organization. However, due to the unique aspects of PS marketing, he will take time to get up to speed.

Line or functional reporting. Having PS marketing report to the corporate marketing organization (or product marketing if there is no corporate marketing group) ensures greater alignment of products and services. On the other hand, if PS marketing reports directly to the PS organization, it tends to be more closely aligned with PS personnel and their needs. The latter is usually the preferred alternative. However, the head of corporate marketing may not be open to having a marketing manager report to someone outside his group. Some PS groups get around this by selecting a creative title to hide the marketing expert in its department.

Reporting to services marketing. Many product-centric companies have a director of services marketing who manages support marketing and education marketing services. On the surface, putting professional services marketing in this organization appears to be a likely choice. However, this can present major challenges because successful marketing strategies and tactics for support, education, and PS vary significantly. The director and his staff must understand the unique nature of each service line of business and ensure the appropriate marketing strategies and tactics are applied accordingly. Expecting support marketing services staff to manage professional services is typically a huge mistake. Support marketing is more similar to product marketing than to professional services marketing.

Marketing staff within the practices. Another organizational decision is whether to put PS marketing resources in remote practices as well as in the corporate office. In a start-up situation, one or more PS marketing staff members are positioned in corporate roles, and the field marketing personnel responsible for products are asked to assist with localizing services marketing materials (e.g., translating marketing materials to the local language) and other services marketing tasks as needed. In a large corporation, services marketing managers may be added in the key geographic practices. But with marketing staff in the remote practices, there is more temptation for each practice to create its own unique services with its own marketing materials, sales tools, and promotion. This dilutes the consistency of the company's services worldwide and the effectiveness of its marketing messages.

Regardless of where the PS marketing personnel are positioned in the company, they will find themselves pulled in many directions—by product marketing, support marketing, PS corporate personnel, and more. PS marketing managers must give priority to the needs of the PS field organization and sales team, and place limits on the time devoted to other headquarters organizations.

Leverage Your Company's Position

When your start a professional services organization, it is important to determine your positioning and document it in a positioning statement. Think about these questions: Who are you? What business are you in? What people do you serve? What business problems do you solve? A good place to begin is to look at your *company and product positioning*. Your customers will automatically associate you with your parent company and will have a hard time believing any perspective that strays too far from the company position. So don't start with a clean slate in positioning your services organization—leverage the position your company already has established in the marketplace.

Ideally, your executive team developed a PS business plan—with a clear mission, goals, and strategies—and gained buy-in from key stakeholders throughout the company. As a marketing manager, you can use the business plan as a base to develop a positioning statement that further communicates your services message throughout your company and to your marketplace.

The goal of positioning is to provide a very clear and concise description of your services business in the customer's mind. You can't be all things to all people—so don't try. Your positioning statement should answer:

- Who is your target market?
- What key problems do your services solve?
- What are your solutions?
- What are the unique benefits your customers derive from your services?
- What differentiates your services from your competitors?

If your organization is small, don't try to hide it. Instead, stress the advantages of greater specialization and expertise, individual attention, and better responsiveness.

A positioning statement ensures clear, consistent communication to your customers. Everyone in your company should be able to articulate your professional services positioning in one or two sentences. The classic test for the length of a positioning statement is the elevator test—can you tell someone what your business is about in the few minutes it takes to ride with them in an elevator?

Success stories and customer references offer credible proof that you deliver unique solutions with clear business benefits as stated in your positioning statement. The stories provide your prospects with a sample of what they can expect if they engage your team.

Importance of a PS Brand Image

As in any business, a PS organization must win customers' hearts and minds by creating a brand image that will attract customers to the business. Brand influences how a customer feels about an offering or a company. Brand can also underscore a company's positioning. Through branding, companies distinguish their offerings from those of their competitors. Many elements work together to build and reinforce a brand: marketing communications, customer relationships, quality, value.

In product companies, marketing managers brand the company and key products or product lines. In services marketing in a product-centric company, the main focus is on branding the PS organization, and secondarily the services methodology. Individual services are rarely branded or trademarked, and even if they are, it will do little good unless the organization brand is effective.

Because services are intangible, a brand is even more important in the services business than it is in a product business. The brand represents everything your services business stands for in the marketplace. Without tangible products to present to a prospect, a brand helps convince people of what you can do and how well you can do it. Services are sold on reputation and trust, and a brand helps establish these qualities in the minds of your prospects. You must manage it and make it work for your organization.

In addition to attracting prospective buyers, a brand helps attract prospective employees. The more alluring your brand, the easier it is to attract the high-quality consultants whom you need to deliver outstanding services.

Let's take a look at some of the elements of a brand strategy.

Brand your organization. Let's start with something as basic as a name. Many professional services organizations don't have a name for themselves. They have a section on the website under "services" or "consulting." You simply cannot create an identity or brand image for your organization without a name to identify it. No one will believe that your company is serious about professional services if your organization doesn't even have a name. Most PS organizations choose a name that leverages their parent company, such as IBM Global Services, HP Services, Sun Professional Services, or BEA Consulting. Your company also must decide if there will be individual brands for consulting, education and support services; one umbrella brand for all services; or brands at both levels.

It is also a good idea to have a *tagline* that clearly positions the organization. A tagline is part of the brand image and reminds customers about the essence of the company. Most car fans know "The Ultimate Driving Machine" used successfully by BMW for years. Or Federal Express' "The world on time." These are catchy, differentiating, and memorable.

Brand your methodology. In addition to branding the organizational name, most PS groups brand their methodology with a name, such as BEA SteelTreads™ Methodology. A large company may brand more than one methodology, in the same way that a large company brands more than one technology. For example, IBM's methodologies include IBM Method BLUE for the implementation and management of enterprise applications, the IBM ALIGN Methodology for server consolidation, and more. It's important to trademark your methodologies. Trademarks call attention and give stature to the methodology, and protect your identity.

Articulate your value proposition. As part of a branding effort, you must create a clear, relevant, and consistent value proposition (that communicates what benefit or worth the customer will get from your services), and marketing messages (that communicate your major themes). For each marketing message, include proof points to add detail and support your message. Your website, collateral, press releases, and other forms of communication leverage your messaging and communicate your value to your customers. Customer success stories are important to establish credibility. Collectively, these materials assist salespeople to foster a positive first impression with prospective customers.

Demonstrate thought leadership. Demonstrate your organization's expertise in specific competencies by holding webinars, speaking at conferences and seminars, and writing articles and whitepapers. In this way, customers can gain an appreciation of your consultants' knowledge and sample the value you can provide to their company. It is one approach to making the intangible tangible.

Align your brand image with your company. The "look and feel" of marketing materials—brochures, service briefs, customer testimonials, white papers, websites, and more—must align with your corporate graphic standards. All customer deliverables for services must be easily identified with your company.

Deliver the promise. Brand image is important, but delivering on your brand's *promise* is even more important. A brand promise sets expectations in the customers' mind. It is your consultants who deliver the service promise and build the company's brand image—or destroy it. The work of your consultants will enable your brand to communicate quality, reliability, sincerity, integrity, and trust—or not. An excellent branding strategy can reinforce the image created by quality services, but it cannot fix an organization whose services do not measure up to the intended brand image.

Building an image for a professional services organization is similar to building an image for a movie star or athlete. Brand can create awareness, but in order to maintain a sustainable advantage the performance of the consultants must be consistent with the expectations set by the brand image. Brand preference is built during the delivery of services. Companies who promise more than they deliver do more harm than good.

Promote your successes. Delivering on the promise results in happy customers, and happy customers provide referrals. Be sure to capture success stories and share them with prospects. If possible, include specific qualitative business results (e.g., enhanced service levels or improved customer relations) and quantitative business results (e.g., the percent increase in IT staff productivity or the percent reduction in IT costs) that can be attributed to your services. Customer referrals are a great way to increase credibility and build your organization's brand.

Extend your company's brand. A brand reflects the soul of the company. In most product-centric companies, it encapsulates the company's products. If your company wants professional services to play a strategic role in your corporation, you must *extend your company brand* to include services. Clearly, the IBM brand stands for both products and services. More companies are also transforming product brands to represent the whole product or the *total solution*—including hardware, software, consulting, education and support, as appropriate.

Ensure Quality Services

Once you have a clear understanding of how your services organization is positioned in the market and your brand's promise, the next question to ask is: How good are your services? Marketing can only enhance the image of a services organization that delivers quality service—it cannot fix a damaged reputation created by poor service delivery.

Product launch. Good product marketing managers do not launch a product and begin sending press releases, ads, or direct mail, until the product has gone through quality assurance, alpha test, and beta test. A product launch begins with a quality product.

Services launch. Likewise, whether your goal is to launch a new competency-based practice or a new service, a PS marketing manager must hold off promotional efforts until the consulting organization is prepared to deliver quality services. Because services-delivery resources are distributed in field offices worldwide instead of being located in headquarters, and services are delivered after they are sold, services marketing managers may not see themselves playing the same role to ensure service quality as the product marketing manager does in confirming product quality. However, promoting a consulting organization that is producing poor quality services only feeds the problem. Even if sales and marketing are successful in attracting customers, they won't remain customers for long if service delivery is flawed. Services marketing managers must ensure that the consulting organization is ready to deliver before launching promotional materials, programs, and events. Otherwise, you may irrevocably damage your brand.

Ensure Adequate Delivery Resources

In addition to managing product quality, companies manage product production ramp-up before general release. Similarly, PS marketing managers must consider how many consultants are qualified to deliver a service line before beginning promotion.

Product launches. When a new product is launched, product marketing wants to generate awareness and create demand. If the budget and resources are available, a product marketing manager may be inclined to launch a product line with a big splash to maximize awareness, and generate as many leads and sales as possible. A product launch frequently includes press releases, advertisements, direct mail literature, email campaigns, collateral, webinars, seminars, sales materials, sales training, and a launch event for customers, analysts, and the press.

Services launches. When launching a new service line, marketing managers must be mindful of the possibility of generating more demand than the PS organization can accommodate at any particular time. The supply/demand dilemma becomes particularly challenging when launching a new area of expertise or competency-based practice. Managers need to consider what skills are required, how many consultants to hire, and how long it will take to find the appropriate consultants and train them. For example, as the security market grows, a company may decide to add security services to its portfolio. Uncertain how fast business can be won in this area, management may be reluctant to grow the staff too quickly. And even if they wanted to grow their new security practice rapidly, it may prove challenging to find the consultants with the right skill set. Some time is required for training even if you hire skilled consultants. Once hired, a consultant's time can be tied up with one customer for months or even years. If you choose to use partners to deliver services, you still need to select partners who have the appropriate skills and level of resources.

Professional services marketing managers face the challenge of how to motivate the sales force without creating more demand than a new PS organization can handle. Engagement managers or other resources skilled in the competency must be available to assist with pre-sales support. And the right talent must be available at the right time to staff engagements. Inability to meet demand can undermine customer loyalty and long-term relationships. For experienced professional services organization, increased demand is welcomed. They have built a partner program and management skills to effectively select, monitor, and measure partners and quickly adapt to marketplace needs.

The flip side of the supply/demand equation—creating more supply than demand—is equally harmful and potentially devastating. Costs go up, and profitability goes down. PS, marketing, and sales must work together to improve demand forecasting and synchronize demand with talent supply. We will address the issue of low utilization in a later chapter.

Start with Marketing Basics

Because services are intangible and cannot be experienced before they are purchased, a prospect's perception of a service is heavily influenced by tangential factors—the dress and personality of the sales team, how the service is presented, and, to some extent, your marketing collateral. Although your marketing materials cannot stand alone in selling your services, they can add or detract from the total "product" perception. Shoddy materials can reflect poorly on the overall professionalism of your company. Be sure your marketing materials enhance your quality image.

Brochures. Brochures do not sell services, and yet you need one to establish credibility and show people that you are serious about being in the PS business. It is your glossy calling card. A good services brochure should have a look and feel that is consistent with other brochures published by your company. It must tell a winning story about your service offerings. One of the most effective ways to do this is to describe the challenges that your target customers face, and the unique solutions your company provides to these problems. Customer testimonial stories and customer quotes are essential to substantiate your message.

Quick reference cards. A quick reference card is another useful sales tool. It provides a more concise description of your consulting business. It typically includes a list of your services; the advantages of your people, methods, and technology; a general overview of how you do business; and whatever else is needed to provide a quick snapshot of your organization. And don't forget the customer quotes. This document is a great summary for customers who are overwhelmed with too much literature to read.

Service briefs. Service briefs—the equivalent of product data sheets —describe service lines or packaged services. Make the look and feel match your company's product data sheets. However, the classic list of features, functions, and specifications included in product data sheets do not apply here. Service briefs describe the customer issues your solutions address, your solution approach, and your specific service offerings. They provide a terrific vehicle to educate your sales reps on your services capabilities. Yet, when meeting with a new prospect, salespeople still need to focus on customer needs. The service briefs are leave-behind marketing collateral. Using them as a tool to describe your services at the beginning of a call can create an impression that you're pushing "products" instead of trying to understand and solve customer problems.

To save cost and facilitate distribution to your sales offices, you may decide to provide service briefs in electronic form instead of investing in printed publications. Then each individual office can print the briefs as needed.

Website. Include your professional services on your company's website. Be sure to include links from your products to related services. And, if your company is truly serious about being in the professional services business, include a link to the services section from your home page.

Position your services in multiple ways. For example, you could present your services by technology areas, business solutions, industries, products, and life cycle phases. One customer may be looking for services related to your servers (product), another may be seeking help with server consolidation (technology), and a third customer may be searching for ways to manage its IT costs (business problem). The solution may end up being the same for all three customers, but their initial approach to the problem may vary. You need to see the world through your customers' eyes in order to position your services appropriately.

Add a little pizzazz to your website, and look for ways to keep visitors returning to the site. Add tips, provocative questions, interesting views from your technical experts, white papers, original research, or anything else that can attract attention.

Build Tools to Support the Sales Team

In addition to providing marketing materials for your customers, create tools to aid salespeople during the professional services sales process. These sales tools will assist your sales team in understanding the who, what, why and how of selling your services. Begin by meeting with PS managers and sales managers. Make sure your sales tools are aligned with your company's sales process.

Sales-ready messaging. Just as a doctor diagnoses a problem before prescribing treatment, the professional services sales process begins with diagnosing the customer's pain and understanding how the problem is impacting the company and the customer. To facilitate this effort, marketing can provide questions to help guide a conversation to uncover issues and needs that your PS organization can solve. A salesperson must understand customer needs to recognize a possible fit and the customer must be in touch with his needs to be open to a discussion about solutions. To get started developing your questions, make a list of needs or problems that your PS organization has solved for customers in each competency area. Talk to PS managers or engagement managers to develop the list.

Once specific needs are discovered, the next step in the sales process is to help the customer visualize a solution, and then finally show how your company's services can provide the desired results. The marketing team can develop scripts or questions that will help the sales team guide the customer in this discovery process—discovering the needs, discovering the possible solutions, and recognizing how your team can provide the best solution. Selling services is a consultative process. Simply talking about the features and benefits of your services will not work. A sales rep must develop a relationship and establish credibility and trust during the sales process. Solution selling will be discussed in more detail in Chapter 9.

Sales guides. Include your sales-ready messaging in a complete sales guide. You can develop sales guides for many different levels of services: all your services, a service line, a packaged service, or a set of services for a particular target market. A sales guide typically includes items such as the ones listed in Table 7.1.

Win tactics. These short stories are both informational and inspirational. They describe the customer environment and give the *specifics* about how a sale was made. They present tips on how to sell professional services and the benefits from a salesperson's perspective. These specifics include steps such as:

- Leverage the long-term relationship with the customer
- Be a global consultancy for a global customer
- Hammer home the superiority of your services
- Form relationships at the executive level
- Focus on value versus price
- Solve the business problem as well as the technical problem

Customer presentations. Consider developing services slides with different levels of information—for your entire PS organization, a service line, or a packaged service (see Table 7.2). Although your sales

TABLE 7.1 Suggested content for a PS sales guide

- Target market for service
- Customer pain points
- Probing questions to ask the prospect
- Qualifiers
- Customer business benefits
- Customer technology benefits
- Sales team benefits
- Service description or service components
- Recommended sales approach
- Competitors and competitive positioning
- Pricing
- Customer references
- Other resources available
- Contacts

and account teams will most likely modify the slides in a presentation to match the customer's needs and their own personal presentation style, it is important to provide a base set of approved slides to alleviate duplication of effort and ensure consistency of messaging. A corporate marketing department can also invest in more professional graphics than a local office can afford to develop.

To create an effective slide presentation, start with the challenges or opportunities faced by the target audience, and then show how your company's services can address these needs. Focus on the *solution* versus simply talking about your company. Adding customer success stories—including customer quotes—from customer projects gives evidence that you have experience in this area and provides credibility to your story. Supplementary slides that speak to the technical problems and your solution approach are useful for presentations to technical managers. Develop notes for each slide for use by the salesperson. Speaking notes can be almost script-like or simply bulleted information that the speaker can present in his own style.

TABLE 7.2 Slide presentations at multiple levels of detail

- High-level PS slides included in your company presentation
- PS slides included in appropriate product-line and product presentations
- PS slides included in a hardware/software/services solution
- PS slides included in your overall services presentation
- PS slide presentation
- PS slide presentation targeting specific audiences
- PS slides describing a service line
- PS slides describing a packaged service

Although presentations have their place, they do not replace the dialogue in a consultative sale. Salespeople need to converse with prospects and understand their needs. Presentations can be helpful in subsequent meetings to communicate your offerings that meet the customer's wants and needs.

Prospect list. Establish a list of prospects from the customers who showed interest in your seminars, webinars, whitepapers, and other documents or events.

Contact list. It is important that your sales team understands what resources are available to aid them in selling consulting services and how they should engage the appropriate players. This information may be included in the sales guide or provided separately on your internal website.

PS dictionary. This document contains a long list of words important to your line of business with brief definitions and reminders for your sales force.

Communications plan. The best way to monitor both external and internal communications materials is to establish a plan. To keep your effort minimal, use a simple table that identifies the activity, audience (internal and external), objectives, schedule, and any other important facets of communications development and delivery. All you need to do weekly or monthly is to fill out a few boxes on the chart.

Align Marketing Materials with the Sales Process

In many companies, a large percentage of marketing and sales materials do not get used by the sales reps. One of the key reasons is that the materials do not align with the way salespeople sell or do not reflect the discussions they are having with their customers. In order to address this problem, marketing managers must do the following:

- Establish a collaborative relationship with the sales organization
- Understand the company's sales process
- Get input from salespeople about collateral and sales tools required
- Get input from salespeople regarding customer problems and needs
- Create value-based messaging that is aligned with customer needs
- Create marketing materials that support the steps in the sales process
- Get feedback on drafts of collateral and sales tools from salespeople before finalizing the materials

If your sales organization is using a consultative or solutions sales approach for products, they will already be focusing on the value of a product or service rather than on its features and functions. However, if your company uses a product-based approach to sales, moving your company to solution-based selling presents a much bigger challenge. We will discuss this topic in the next chapter.

Make Your Consultants Stars

Customers hire consultants because they are experts. The job of your marketing department is to help establish your consultants as thought leaders. Demonstrate your organization's competence by letting the consultant's expertise speak for itself. The more complex the service, the more important it is to build customers' confidence in the consultants delivering these high-end services. Let's look at some of the top ways to accomplish this.

Speaking engagements. One of the best ways to demonstrate your consultants' expertise is to have them present to groups of prospective customers. For broader visibility, speaking engagements at technology or industry meetings is an excellent forum. Most high-tech companies have user groups and hold annual meetings at one or more locations around the world. Find opportunities for your consultants to present at these meetings.

At the end of the presentation, be sure to include the address of your website or other information so people can contact you for further discussion. If possible, find a way to make yourself available to meet with interested parties at the event. Direct them to your booth, host a small party in the evening, or simply state where you will be available after the presentation.

Seminars. Seminars are another excellent way of establishing credibility. They can be either small-scale seminars or large seminars. Because small seminars are more intimate, you are more likely to get prospects to discuss their challenges. Select a topic that is both related to your competencies and of interest to the invited executives. Include some of your past customers who can share their experiences working with your organization. Invite a respected individual to speak for about 30-45 minutes or have someone from your group present. Then open the topic for discussion. This can be done with the entire group if it is a small gathering. Or the group can be subdivided into smaller teams with someone from your organization facilitating discussions in each subgroup. The goal is to get the attendees talking about how the topic relates to issues in their business. If you have formed subgroups, you may want to bring the entire group together toward the end and have the subgroups share their discussions. You will learn more about ways you can assist the customers. Participants will benefit by learning from each other as well as becoming aware of your consulting organization's capabilities.

Large seminars or workshops can also be effective if properly managed. Years ago, Cambridge Technology Partners did an excellent job of gaining customers through seminars. They held free seminars for executives that discussed solutions and how applications could be developed quickly. They followed this with fee-based workshops where developers created a prototype of an application. The goal was to sell custom consulting to build and test the application. The free seminars created the forum needed to sell the value to company decision makers and to get them excited about having Cambridge assist them to produce results quickly.

Whether large or small, the corporate marketing department can assist the local consulting practices by creating the content and materials for workshops. This may include sample invitations, agendas, and presentations. To take advantage of accomplished speakers, organize a roadshow in which a team of speakers travels from city to city to present at the local seminars.

Webinars. Another good way to help establish your consultants as thought leaders is to schedule webinars about topics of interest to your target markets. Ask your consultants to present at the webinars. Invite customers and prospects to listen to your webinars at no charge. Tape the webinars and make them available on your website. Whether listeners call into the initial live webinar or listen to the recorded version, capture their contact information and present the leads to your sales force.

Published documents. Consultants can also demonstrate their expertise by writing about their technology approaches. They could publish articles in trade magazines and newspapers read by perspective customers. Set a goal for each senior consultant to write a number of articles every year. Consider offering a bonus to provide an incentive. Hire writers to either interview the consultants to obtain content for articles and write the articles, or polish drafts written by the consultants. On your website, provide links to the published articles. To further leverage articles, produce reprints and distribute them to corporate and remote offices for a variety of uses.

Publishing books is another means of touting the knowledge of your organization. If writing a book is too ambitious, create white papers to establish your expertise on a topic. Most white papers present a fairly vendor-neutral approach to a topic and then include a short advertisement at the end about the company's expertise in providing products and services relating to the topic. Your consultants can write white papers for both management and technical audiences. Distribute articles and white papers on your website or as part of the portfolio of materials you share with prospective customers. Also use them as handouts after a presentation.

Newsletters. Distribute a weekly or monthly email newsletter packed with useful tips from your consultants. Use it to promote upcoming seminars, webinars, or other events where your consultants will be speaking. Announce new white papers or success stories. Interview a customer and share his comments about how the engagement benefited his company. Share a few best practices related to your competencies.

Deliver value. All of these approaches—speaking engagements, seminars, published documents, newsletters—include giving something to the prospect (e.g., new ideas, thoughts, direction). Each approach demonstrates the knowledge of your consultants and how they can be of service to customers. This pull-marketing approach is considerably more effective than having your marketing people proclaim the virtues of your organization. It also allows consultants to make a valuable contribution to the organization when they are not working on an engagement.

To sell professional services, you need to meet with the customer to understand his needs, help him visualize a solution, and convince him that your organization can provide the desired solution. People are much more likely to meet with a company that they are aware of and respect. Use the methods discussed above to create awareness and provide samples of your value. Hopefully, these prospects then will contact you. Or at least they will welcome a meeting when your sales team calls.

Turn Successes into References

One of the most important ways to demonstrate your organization's expertise is to let your customers tell your story. Your customers may not believe your marketing department, and may even be somewhat skeptical of your consultants touting their expertise, but they will be especially receptive to credible opinions from other customers. The closer you can relate to a customer's situation the better. Industry success stories, technology success stories, and solution success stories are extremely valuable. If applicable, include information on services in your product success stories, too. You can't have too many customer references.

In your success stories, describe the customer's challenges, your solutions, and the benefits. In addition to discussing technical issues, be sure to describe the business implications of the issues, such as excessive costs, reduced productivity, or non-compliance with federal regulations. Likewise, when describing the benefits, include tangible business benefits with quantifiable results. To promote significant engagements, consider developing case studies that include a more in-depth analysis of the business drivers, solution details, and business value with substantial quantitative information. Case studies provide a powerful way to demonstrate the cost effectiveness of your services.

It is valuable to include short success stories and customer quotes in brochures, service briefs, press releases, and advertisements. They add an element of credibility to all your marketing and sales materials.

Using two- or three-minute video segments of customers telling their story is also effective in seminars and presentations.

Professional services organizations frequently offer the same technical services to clients in all industries. However, in some cases, managers would prefer to hire consultants with expertise in their particular industry. Large technology companies, such as IBM, can afford to offer services that are targeted to particular industries, along with consultants who bring industry expertise. Medium-sized companies may find it profitable to establish industry practices in key locations for select industries that are most important to their business. And all companies, regardless of size, should develop customer reference stories related to their key industries.

Success stories are an excellent way to promote your organization internally and educate and motivate salespeople. When I was a marketing manager at Sun Professional Services, we had a program called "The Customer of the Week." Every week, we selected the most successful completed engagement and broadcast a conference call between the VP of Professional Services and the engagement team, including the account sales representative. In this way, we acknowledged the work done by the consultants, provided internal visibility to key successes, and allowed the sales team to hear their peers talk about how the engagement contributed to the customer relationship and resulted in increased revenues. Salespeople are much more likely to believe other salespeople than your marketing staff. We posted the audio tapes of the broadcasts and the transcription of the meetings on the internal web so PS personnel or sales representatives could access them at their convenience. This program was well-received within the professional services organization, as well as other parts of the company.

What Doesn't Work

Mass marketing techniques, such as direct mail, email blasts, and advertising, do not work in selling services. The only exception may be in selling very low-end, inexpensive services. Anything else requires a face-to-face meeting with the prospect. Because most services are customized for the customer, all the necessary information cannot be captured without sitting down together and understanding the customer's needs. Even packaged services are not likely to sell through direct mail or Internet based marketing. However, direct mail, email, or telemarketing may be effective in *introducing* packaged services or solutions to specific target audiences, or inviting prospects to seminars, webinars, workshops, or other events where your consultants are speaking.

At one corporation, which primarily marketed to large enterprises, a decision was made at a high level to make all products and services available for purchase on the company's website. No sales contact would be required. To comply, the consulting organization was required to include all the packaged services. Not only did this approach expose professional services pricing and statement of works to the competition, the efforts produced no positive results— the company never received one order for consulting services via the Web. Once again, what works for products, doesn't necessarily work for services.

Remember: It's about People

Whether you are creating a brochure, a service brief, a success story, or any other marketing publication, it is important to remember that your customers are buying the expertise of your consultants. One of my pet peeves is services marketing literature that talks about the consulting business as if everything is bundled in little boxes and these packages show up at your doorstep to do the work. These documents say "the performance service does this, the implementation service does that, etc." This approach works for inanimate hardware and software, but not for services. Instead, try "our consultants assess your IT organization" or "our architects work side-by-side with your software development team" or "we have decades of experience in optimizing the performance of high-end servers." Be proud of your consultants and extol their knowledge and experience.

Instead of describing individual services, it is a good idea to group services into service lines. An effective document describing a service line focuses on customer problems, your approach to solving the problems, the expertise your consultants offer in this area, and the customers you have helped. Make sure your prospects know that you bring highly qualified, professional experts to the table and not a bunch of robots. Use words like: our approach, our consultants, our security experts, our methodology, our technology, or we employ a four-step process. Don't take the people out of your services—you devalue your services by presenting them as if anyone can do the job.

Make It Easy to Find Your Services

Your PS organization is selling expertise that comes in many different flavors. How do you get your sales force and your prospects to understand what flavors you offer and how your services align with their needs?

Each customer starts the search for services from a different perspective. Let's take the example of security services. One manager may be looking for someone who can evaluate the overall IT security risks to his company. Another may be searching for expertise relating to a specific security product. Still another may be looking for help with security for an e-commerce solution. A banking manager may be seeking help with security as it relates to his company's banking applications. And another banking manager may be looking for an organization to assume responsibility for managing the security operations for his company.

Common approaches that prospects use to search for high-tech services include:

- By product
- By technology

- By business solutions
- By industry
- By service lifecycle

Position the company's services so it is easy for customers—as well as for salespeople and other internal staff—to locate offerings. It's worth the time and effort. To get ideas on how to categorize your company's services, visit some of your competitors' websites. At the time this book was written, IBM grouped its services in the following ways:

- By industry (e.g., automotive, banking, financial markets, healthcare, insurance, retail)
- By business issue (e.g., streamline business processes, optimize IT investments)
- By business consulting area (e.g., customer relationship management, supply chain management, financial management)
- By hardware/software platform (e.g., desktops, operating systems, storage software)
- By market size (e.g., small business, medium business)
- By alphabetical listing of services

After drafting categories for your services, ask practice managers, engagement managers, others in your field consulting practices, and your sales organization for comments. Industry analysts are also a valuable resource to review your proposed categories. In addition to the groupings, reviewers can provide input on your terminology. Sometimes a company uses a label in one way, not realizing that its definition is unique to its corporation and has little meaning to the wider marketplace. An industry analyst can point out market issues with the terms you've created.

Using pull-down menus on your website, you can present your services in multiple categories. This makes it easy for prospects to locate the groups of services that most interest them. Also, be sure to include links from your product web pages to related services that offer product installation, configuration, implementation, integration, operation, and other product assistance.

Whatever way you choose to present your services, make sure that the categories and terminology are used consistently in your printed collateral, intranet and Internet sites, presentations, sales guides, and other internal and customer materials. Investing the time in clear service positioning will facilitate the learning process for everyone in your company, strengthen your brand, and make it easier for prospects to understand how your services and solutions can best support their needs.

Stacking Up Against the Competition

Professional services organizations must be aware of the competitive companies that are providing similar services. Competitive information may be gained from the following sources:

- Competitors' websites
- Publicly available marketing collateral
- Industry analyst reports
- Salespeople and engagement managers involved in sales opportunities

Competitive pricing information—for both custom services and packaged services—is the data that is most desired. It is also the most difficult information to obtain. The prices are not usually published, and even if they were, it is difficult to compare your services with those of your competitors.

In general, it is more challenging to find competitive information on services than on products. Analysts provide more reports on products than services—although that is changing to some degree. Because products are concrete, the features and functions can easily be found on websites and in published data sheets. In contrast, the custom nature of most services makes it difficult to conduct a price comparison of service offerings.

However, the good news is that competitive analysis is less critical in services marketing than in product marketing. Customers evaluate a company's people, processes, and technologies. They are initially influenced by the consulting organization's reputation. After meeting with the consulting personnel, the expertise demonstrated in the sales cycle and the relationships formed make a difference in winning the business. Prospective customers do not do a point-by-point comparison of alternative consulting groups or services. The selection process is often more of a feeling than a pure technical analysis.

Rather than spending a great deal of effort on competitive analysis, more benefit can be obtained from win-loss analysis. Why are you winning deals? Why are you losing deals? Who is the competition? What is the size of the deal? For opportunities that you win, what are the factors that the sales team believes most contributed to the win?

You can also conduct a survey or focus group to see how your customers or companies in your markets rate your services and prices compared to your competitors.

Marketing inside the Company

Within a product company, a product marketing manager interfaces with a management team, marketing staff, sales organization, and the development or engineering team who understand products and the product business. A PS marketing manager also often interfaces with this same team who understands products and the product business— not services, or the professional services business. As a PS marketing manager, the words I heard most often from other services marketing people about our peers in the product sector of the business were "they just don't get it." This means that the services manager is faced with a huge challenge of marketing services and educating people inside the company.

Let's take a look at the audiences who need to buy into services.

Management. Managers say they are behind services, but often fail to allocate adequate resources to the business. PS marketing managers must educate management in order to obtain an adequate marketing budget. The budget for services marketing is usually about three percent of services revenue.

Marketing. Most of the marketing personnel in the company understand products—not services. And yet, PS marketing managers are often dependent on product marketing specialists in marcom, public relations, and other areas for assistance. In turn, a large team of product specialists will frequently be calling on services marketing for input to launches, materials, and events. In order for these relationships to work, the product marketing resources must understand and value services.

One challenge for some PS marketing managers is getting professional services information into corporate brochures and product data sheets. Although the corporation may be committed to consulting services, there are frequently territorial issues that arise among the marketing managers. As a result, services are often slighted in product and company literature. There should be a company-wide policy that services are mentioned in all external product communications.

Sales. PS marketing managers are totally dependent on the sales organization or third-party sales channels to close business, so the marketing team must help educate and motivate the sales team to sell services. Sales relationships are particularly important in professional services sales because people do not buy custom consulting services—or even most packaged services—without meeting face-to-face with someone to discuss their problems or opportunities and the potential solutions. PS marketing managers can assist salespeople by aligning tools wih the solution selling process, including questions that guide the conversation and uncover customer wants and needs that your PS organization can solve.

Consultants. One of the best ways to find new projects is during the delivery of an engagement. Consultants must appreciate this opportunity and take advantage of it. Marketing managers can help prepare consultants to market services. To be successful marketing services to customers, services marketing managers must first be successful in internal marketing.

Summary

PS marketing is different from product marketing. You need marketing managers who understand the unique aspects of marketing professional services—and, ideally, marketing people with experience working in a product-centric company. The most effective way to position your organization is to leverage your company and product positioning. Brand your organization and your methodology—not your services.

Mass marketing techniques—such as direct mail, advertising, and brochures—produce limited or no results in selling services. Develop sales-ready messaging to facilitate a consultative sales approach. Establish thought leadership through seminars, webinars, white papers, and articles. And, best of all, let your customers tell your story. Customer references top the list of effective marketing techniques for services.

Questions for Consideration

Does your company understand how to market services?

Any marketing manager who makes the transition from products to services learns very quickly that the approach and programs used for products does not work effectively in marketing professional services. Here are some topics to consider when evaluating your services marketing effectiveness.

- Where does your services marketing staff fit in your organization?
    - Do you have resources dedicated to PS marketing?
    - Does PS marketing report to corporate marketing, product marketing, services marketing, or directly to the professional services organization?
    - Are your PS marketing personnel experienced in marketing consulting services in a product-centric company?

- Is your organization well positioned?
    - Is the positioning tied to your parent company?
    - Can everyone in PS, as well as your sales organization, articulate your service positioning?

- Do you have a clear and effective brand image to attract customers?
    - Does your organization deliver quality work in order to provide a solid foundation to build a quality image and reputation? Do you deliver what you promise?
    - Does your professional services organization have a name?
    - Do you have a branded name for your methodology?
    - Do you have a clear value proposition?

- How would you describe the overall image of your PS organization from the perspective of your target markets, your current customers, and your own company—especially the sales team?

- What programs do you use to promote your organization and your services and create thought leadership?
  - Do you have customer success stories? Are your customers willing to speak to prospects?
  - Do your consultants speak at technology or industry meetings?
  - Do you hold seminars to discuss your solution areas?
  - Do you publish articles, white papers, press releases, or books?

- Are your services mapped into well-defined categories?
  - By product
  - By technology
  - By business solutions
  - By industry
  - By service lifecycle

- Are your professional services presented consistently in all your printed collateral, intranet and Internet sites, presentations, sales guides, and other sales and marketing materials?

- Are the terms used to label your service categories well understood within your industry and by your target customers?

- How do you stack up against your competition?
  - Who are your competitors?
  - Do you gather win-loss information and analyze this data to understand where, why, and how you are winning or losing business?

- How effective is your internal marketing?

  o   Do your management team, product marketing team, sales organization, and consultant organization understand your services and how they are positioned?

- Does your PS marketing organization have a collaborative relationship with the sales organization?

  o   Do your marketing people understand the sales process used by your sales team?

  o   Has your marketing team surveyed the sales team to get feedback on whether the services marketing materials are being used, how they are used, and if the materials meet its needs?

  o   Do the PS marketing materials map to the steps in the sales process?

  o   Are sales tools available to help the sales rep evaluate customer needs and business pains and map your solutions to the customer's issues?

8

Establish a PS Sales Force

*Build a professional services sales team
and align it with your product sales team.*

When a company has a recognized need for consultants, it calls the firms that have expertise in the desired solution area and an established reputation for doing quality work. Evidence of your expertise—customer testimonials, awards, press clippings, white papers, original research—will help get you in the prospect's door. Your sales team then must create a relationship of trust in order to win the business.

Demonstrating an understanding of the customer's problem, presenting credible alternative solutions, and discussing your experience in solving similar problems are all ways to build credibility. Each meeting and presentation should be designed to increase the level of trust. Depending upon the size and complexity of the project, it may take some time for the prospect to believe that your team truly understands his problem and has the knowledge and experience to solve it in the timeframe needed. The professional services sales process is a courtship, building trust and forming the basis for a commitment to do business together.

Don't Bet on Product Salespeople

Most high-tech companies have their own direct sales force. When you launch a professional services organization, it seems logical to select this sales group to sell services. There are advantages to this choice. The product sales force has contacts within your customer base, has established a relationship with your customers, and hopefully understands their needs. Despite these advantages, most product salespeople in high-tech companies are not successful in selling services, in particular without special training.

People don't buy services in the same way they buy products. Likewise, sales reps cannot effectively sell services in the same way they sell products. Most product salespeople lead with one of the company's products. They describe the features and functions of the product, as well as the ways it is superior to the competition. However, as we discussed in Part I, people buy services based on expertise, reputation, and trust, and not on features, functions, price, and competition.

I don't mean to imply that you can't teach an old salesperson new tricks—just that it takes time, training, and patience—and he must be willing to learn. Even with training, some sales representatives will be unable or unwilling to change their sales approach.

Typically, about 10 percent of a company's product sales force will succeed in selling services. But there are methods, such as "solution selling," that are designed to increase these odds. These methods require sales training, support from the marketing organization, and commitment at the top.

The more complex your products, the more likely your sales force will already have the skills required to sell professional services because the challenges are similar. Both have a long sales cycle and succeed better with a direct sales team, heavy involvement of people with expert knowledge, compelling success stories, and selling high in the organization. Companies selling complex products are most likely employing a solution selling approach. (Solution selling will be discussed in Chapter 9.)

Don't Bet on Support Services Reps

An alternative to using product salespeople is to charter the already-existing services sales organization that sells traditional support and educational offerings to sell consulting services. Although it may seem natural to group professional services with support services, this approach is even less likely to succeed than counting on product salespeople. First, support representatives are usually brought in at the end of the product sales cycle, when the opportunity for assessments, systems architecture, design, and many other professional services has passed. Second, support representatives typically have less of a big-picture understanding of the customer's environment and needs than product salespeople. They also tend to call on lower-level people in the organization.

Create an Overlay Sales Team

The most successful strategy for selling professional services is to create a sales force consisting of sales account managers who oversee the relationship with key accounts, and overlay sales teams who may be called on for their deeper product, services, or industry knowledge. The overlay personnel can be product representatives or professional services representatives. However, this structure is only cost effective for large corporations or for large strategic accounts in medium-sized companies.

Sales account manager. The account manager, as the primary sales contact for a key account, understands the customer's business, and also has a general understanding of his own company's products and services. Instead of a "box" selling technique, highlighting "speeds and feeds," the account manager focuses on relationship selling. He concentrates his efforts on the overall business relationship with the customer organization. This requires a blend of technical savvy, exemplary communication skills, business acumen, and long-term customer management skills.

Product representatives. When specific product needs arise, the account manager calls on product representatives. These specialists bring deep knowledge in particular product lines or technologies. Alternatively, these overlay reps may be aligned with distinct customer segments, such as manufacturing enterprises or the SMB market segment, instead of product lines. Whatever their specialty, product representatives should have the expertise to understand customer issues, conduct in-depth discussions, communicate product features and benefits, demonstrate products, share product success stories, and give product presentations.

PS representatives. When consulting needs arise, the account manager brings in a professional services representative. Using a consultative sales approach, the overlay PS representative can engage the customer in an in-depth conversation regarding his needs, present alternative solutions to meet the needs, and guide the customer to see clearly how your services provide an ideal solution. The PS representative is expert in helping customers envision how they can use technology—and your services—to increase the effectiveness and efficiency of their business.

This sales team (account manager, product representatives, and PS representatives) develops and proposes solutions to address a customer's overall needs. It is essential for the PS salesperson to develop a solid relationship with the principal account manager and demonstrate how PS can add value to the sales process. Bringing the team of salespeople together in the same sales training and meetings can foster team building.

IBM is one—if not *the most*—effective high-tech company at building and managing sales teams. It was IBM's mastery of direct sales that drove it to dominance in the 1960s and 1970s. And its continued expertise in selling solutions plays a large part in its success in the professional services business. IBM's sales approach is centered around sales account managers teaming with overlay sales representatives.

Divide and Conquer Doesn't Work

Some companies that believe they aren't large enough to justify having account managers with overlay product sales representatives and PS sales representatives, simply add a professional services sales team. The product sales team reports to the product organization, and the PS sales team reports to the professional services organization. This makes two sales organizations calling on the same prospects. Trust me—it doesn't work.

With this approach, the company presents two faces to the customer, and the customer becomes confused. Competition can arise between the two organizations. As a result, the product organization may even develop stronger partnerships with systems integrators and value-added retailers than with its own company's services organization.

If you have a product sales force and decide to add a professional services sales force, it is highly recommended that both groups report into the same sales organization. The PS salespeople should be closely aligned and integrated with the product salespeople. Ideally, all salespeople should be trained in and following a common sales process. If you use different sales methods for the product sales team and the PS sales team, you must integrate the two methods and cross-train the sales organizations. All those calling on an account must see themselves as one team with a united sales strategy, presenting one unified face to the customer.

Instead of creating a new sales organization, many companies hire business development managers (BDMs) to assist in selling professional services. BDMs are generally tasked with assessing target markets and market opportunities, gathering intelligence on customers and competitors, generating leads, qualifying prospects, and writing formal proposals.

Regardless of whether you create a full-fledged PS sales organization or hire business development managers to assist with selling professional services, be sure that the team is closely aligned with your product sales team.

Invest in Solution Selling Training

If you decide to charter your company's product sales force to sell professional services, the sales team must make the difficult shift from product selling to solution selling. To be successful in introducing solution selling, it first takes a commitment by sales management to invest the time and money in training the sales reps, and then another commitment to implement the recommended process.

Mike Bosworth offers his version of the solution selling sales process in his book *Solution Selling*.[9] The process encompasses pre-call planning, creating interest, diagnosing the problem, vision processing, controlling the sales, closing, and post-sales tracking. Michael Bosworth has also co-authored a more recent book entitled *Customer Centric Selling*[10] that describes the process.

The goal of Customer Centric Selling is to help the customer solve a problem, satisfy a need, or achieve a goal. It requires engaging the customer in conversations, guiding him to realize his goal, exploring how the problem is impacting the company and its customers, visualizing a solution, and seeing the benefits of the solution. Instead of developing presentations to pitch offerings, marketing managers create "Sales-Ready Messaging" to assist salespeople through the process.

Once a salesperson has successfully helped the prospect visualize the solution, she has now earned the right to present how the company's services can provide the desired solution. Just as a doctor needs to take the time to ask questions to diagnose a patient's problem before offering a prescription, your sales team needs to ask questions, patiently listen, and avoid jumping in too quickly to offer solutions. The process is most effective when the customer reaches his own conclusion.

Solution Selling® eLearning curriculum and instructor-led workshops are provided by authorized trainers throughout the world. Check the Web to find a trainer in your area.

---

9.   Michael T. Bosworth, *Solution Selling: Creating Buyers in Difficult Selling Markets*, McGraw-Hill, 1995.

10.   Michael T. Bosworth and John R. Holland, *Customer Centric Selling*, McGraw-Hill, 2003.

Provide Motivation and Incentives

In addition to knowing *how* to sell services, sales representatives must be *motivated* to sell services. Salespeople in product companies joined the enterprise with the skills and desire to sell products. If a sales rep is already making significant commissions by selling hardware or software, he may not be motivated to sell services. Convincing the sales representatives of the value of selling services can present a challenge. And if your sales force isn't committed to the PS program, it isn't going to work no matter how extraordinary your consultants and services.

Each salesperson's compensation typically consists of a base salary plus commission (bonus). So providing commissions for selling services is an essential motivator. Although providing incentives may appear obvious, it is amazing how many product companies resist taking this step. If your products are very high priced and your services tend to be significantly lower priced in comparison, a higher commission percentage on services may be required to sufficiently motivate your sales representatives—especially during the first 6 to 12 months. And sometimes even a higher commission doesn't provide enough inducement for some salespeople to learn new selling skills and to understand the service offerings.

One of the best incentives is to require salespeople to meet a services sales quota to qualify for the company's top sales club. Of course, for this to be taken seriously, it must be enforced without exceptions. This shows that top management is truly committed to making professional services an integral part of the business.

PS Pre-Sales Support Must "Walk the Talk"

Practice managers, engagement managers, and other field personnel who are involved in delivering services are in an excellent position to help market and sell services. They are closest to the customer. They have the best understanding of customer needs. They can tell firsthand stories to prospects about projects conducted for other customers. They have the knowledge and experience to relate to the customer's problems, recommend alternative solutions, help the customer select the best solution, and discuss similar solutions your organization provided for other companies. And an extra bonus is that they are in a position to influence the customer's future services purchases.

First-hand experience with consulting engagements is invaluable. I am familiar with a company where the PS business development team was staffed with experienced MIS managers who were not experienced with selling or delivering services. They were hired with the understanding that they could relate to the customer's needs and thus be successful. In most cases, they merely served as another layer for the customer to go through before a practice manager or an engagement manager was brought into the account to discuss the customer's needs and alternative solutions.

To provide optimal pre-sales support, use engagement managers to the best advantage. One way is to increase their numbers and call on them to support PS sales efforts, while continuing to manage consulting engagements. To maintain a sustainable balance, sales support requests must be managed properly. Another approach is to create a career path for your engagement managers into PS sales. In either case, you can feel confident that engagement managers can help the customer envision how your services will solve his technical and business problems.

Teamwork and Trust Between Sales and PS

A good relationship between the sales force and PS is essential to successfully sell consulting services. Practice managers, engagement managers, and other PS resources involved in the sales process must mentor the sales representatives to help them understand the professional services business. Salespeople must trust PS.

Freebies to customers, account management, and alignment between marketing and sales are three areas where sales and PS must learn to understand each other's viewpoints and create win-win strategies.

Freebies. Salespeople are often seduced by the customer into providing free consulting or offering significant discounts without PS approval—especially when selling services that pull through product. One way to handle this is to require your sales organization to pay PS for a service that is provided for free or discounted. This way, the sales organization doesn't impact the profitability of the PS organization. And sales management can decide whether the potential opportunity is significant enough to warrant services funding.

Account management. Good salespeople are used to being in control of their accounts. They take pride in understanding their customer's business and its challenges, building strong and productive relationships, and winning customer loyalty. An engagement team living at the customer site changes the dynamics. Some sales reps may see the PS account team as a threat to their account control. The engagement team and sales team must collaborate to develop an account plan for successfully managing the interactions and relationships with the customer.

In the ideal situation, the sales rep understands and appreciates the contributions that the account team makes to account management. One sales representative told me how the PS team on his account provides account control and account protection. He said, "Often there is an internal meeting about a problem at a customer site and the customer will blame the problem on the vendor that is not in the room to defend itself. As a sales rep, I have five pairs of eyes and ears on site that are helping solve problems and sell hardware." In that account, there was clearly a successful alliance between sales and PS that resulted in strong customer satisfaction and significant services revenue.

Marketing and sales alignment. Close alignment between the PS sales organization and the PS marketing organization is a must. Collaboration takes some effort, but in the long run it's a great route to productive selling. Some ways for marketing to create alignment with sales include the following:

- Attend sales meetings
- Join the sales teams on calls and meetings with prospects
- Set up training classes on solution selling and selling your company's services
- Design marketing materials to match the phases of the sales cycle
- Create sales tools to facilitate an understanding of customer needs and how your services can provide the desired results

Identifying Prospects

To attract highly qualified prospects, your marketing organization can establish thought leadership through speaking engagements, seminars, webinars, and other methods that demonstrate the knowledge of your consultants and how they can be of service. However, the best place to start looking for consulting opportunities is with your existing customers.

Sell to existing customers. There are many reasons why existing customers usually represent the best source for new business.

Established relationships. People like to do business with people they know. They want an ongoing relationship with someone who understands them and cares about them. During the delivery of professional services, the day-to-day interaction with the customer naturally fosters a relationship. If your team performs the service well, you earn the customer's confidence and trust. They know you deliver value. They know you are trustworthy.

When a new project arises, if your team has performed well in the past, you are most likely to win the new business without the need to compete against any contenders. Even if your skills are not an exact match with the project needs, the customer will most likely give the opportunity to a team he knows and trusts, rather than an unknown source that claims to have a greater level of expertise. Although people also develop loyalty to products, the personal relationships formed during service delivery generate an even greater level of customer loyalty.

Cost/price advantages. Studies show that it can cost five times more to acquire new customers than keep current customers. Because the customer already knows and understands what you can offer, your marketing costs are lower. Your team has proven it can deliver quality results on time and on schedule. When a customer develops a strong relationship with the service provider and values the work performed in the past, the customer is more likely to pay a premium price for future services.

Quicker ramp-up. Once the project is won, the delivery team requires less time to get up to speed on understanding the customer and industry. The relationships have already been formed. There is an understanding of how the customer likes to do business and manage projects. The PS organization has already invested the time to understand the customer's business problems and organizational dynamics.

Together, all of the above factors mean that follow-up engagements are often more profitable than first-time engagements.

Solidify relationships with customers. Your engagement team must realize that its performance on a project can determine whether or not your company is selected for additional projects with the customer. Performing the project extremely well and meeting time and budget commitments are the minimum requirements for a ticket to work with this customer on a future project.

Managing expectations. In order to meet the dual goals of achieving customer satisfaction and providing a profit for PS, the engagement team must exceed the customer's expectations without giving away the store. This starts with setting clear expectations that are both agreed upon orally as well as documented in a statement of work. Once an understanding is established, any deviance from the agreement must be documented in a change order. Lack of good change management procedures is a common cause of mismanaged expectations as well as lower project profitability. The engagement manager's challenge is to help the customer feel that his expectations have been exceeded without sacrificing the expected profitability from the project.

Brag when appropriate. Broadcasting milestone successes plays a role in capturing your customer for repeat business. If a technical manager is super pleased with a report, the customer hiring manager should know about it. If your milestone is completed under the cost projection or a deadline is beaten, your project manager should communicate this to your customer management. They are usually aware when things are not going well. On the other hand, the customer often needs to be reminded when he is getting what was promised.

Keep communicating. Practice managers and business development managers should phone the customer frequently and take the time to visit the customer. They should make sure the project and the relationship are going well. Don't assume that the lack of grievances means the project is going well. In fact, the lack of complaints is more likely a sure sign of impaired communications and a declining relationship. If a customer's frustrations accumulate over time, instead of being expressed, they could lead to serious relationship problems that may prove difficult or costly to fix. Communicate well and frequently.

Increase your customer knowledge. Really knowing your customer is flattering to him and useful to you. Get to know the customer's organization, business, and industry. Read brochures and annual reports and follow the news about the customer. Ask your customer to draw you an organization chart and use it to identify the key prospects in the customer's organization and arrange to meet with these managers. After learning about a department's wants and needs, develop a plan for winning the customer's additional business. Provide white papers or give presentations to demonstrate your expertise. Share customer success stories to show how you were able to solve similar problems for other customers.

After a project is completed, stay in touch with the customer. Invite the customer to your customer visitor center to meet your company president and other executives. Help your customer get to know other managers in your company.

Identify additional business. While working at an account, the engagement team constantly needs to be on the lookout for evidence of new challenges. Identify what the customer is doing well and where improvement is needed. Then point out how your company can address the weaknesses. Assessment services provide an effective means to accomplish this diagnosis. All projects should end with a discussion or formal proposal about additional ways that PS is able to assist the customer.

To increase the odds of additional work, the entire team must invest in the customer relationship. Be cooperative and responsive throughout the project. Go the extra mile. Make your customers feel important.

Sell to new customers. Although existing PS customers are the lifeblood of the organization, it is dangerous to rely too much on a few customers. If a customer runs into financial hard times, consultants may be the first to be cut. To keep your organization thriving, new customers must continually be added. Also, through new business, PS expands its industry knowledge, skills, and references.

PS marketing can lead the sales cycle by building a brand image through references and communications that demonstrate your expertise and broadcasts your capabilities to your markets. Once awareness has been established, market segments can be influenced by a series of organized events that gradually create interest in your company. Marketing managers can compile a list of prospects it has reached through marketing campaigns. Customers are best won by a slow courting process of face-to-face dialogues where they get to know you better.

Summary

Most product sales representatives are not successful in selling services. If you are a large corporation, consider creating an overlay sales team with PS representatives to help sell professional services. Smaller companies may decide to hire business development managers to support PS sales. If you decide to use your product sales force to sell services, be sure to invest in sales training and incentives. Engage practice managers, engagement managers, and other field personnel who are involved in delivering services to assist in the sales process.

Questions for Consideration

How effective is your sales organization in selling consulting services?

Product companies know how to sell products. Selling consulting services or total solutions presents one of the biggest hurdles that product companies face in achieving success in the services business. To diagnose how your company can become more effective in selling professional services, consider the following questions.

- How is your PS sales organization structured?
  - Do you have an account sales manager assigned to key accounts who brings in product and services specialists, including overlay PS sales reps, as needed?
  - If not, do you have PS sales reps whom your product salespeople can call on when needed? Do both PS and product sales teams report into the same sales organization?
  - Do your PS sales reps have experience as engagement managers or other experience that qualifies them to relate to your customer's problems, present alternative solutions, and discuss similar services provided to other customers?

- Does your PS group have a good relationship with your product and services sales reps?
  - Does PS have a good reputation with your sales team?
  - Do product sales reps understand how to identify services opportunities and know when to bring in PS sales reps or other PS personnel to assist with the sales process?
  - Are PS personnel available to assist the sales team when requested?
  - Are practice managers, engagement managers, or other PS experts brought into new sales situations early enough in the process to be effective?

- o   Does PS marketing work effectively with the sales team to support its sales needs?

- How effective is your company at selling to existing customers?
  - o   Are the customers' expectations well managed?
  - o   Does the PS team effectively communicate its accomplishments?
  - o   Is the engagement team skillful in identifying new opportunities and communicating your company's expertise and success stories with similar challenges?
  - o   How would you rate your company's reputation with your customers?

- How effective is your sales organization at bringing in new business?
  - o   Is your sales team effective in matching a prospect's challenges and opportunities with your services and solution offerings?
  - o   What approaches do you use to communicate your expertise and successes to new prospects?

9

Manage the Sales Process

*A well-defined sales process—including qualification,
proposal development, and contract management—helps
you identify opportunities and close engagements.*

A large, complex systems integration project may require 30 or 40 consultants or more, span many months or even years, and entail a fair amount of risk. The larger the project, the greater the risk. To mitigate risk and win and close engagements, a consulting organization needs a well-defined sales process. Carefully managing the process ensures that customer requirements are thoroughly analyzed, appropriate resources are available for the customer project, and the project is priced to produce the expected profit.

A large project provides the potential for large profits and positive references—or large losses and negative word of mouth. The work required to ensure success instead of failure begins with the sales process—qualification, proposal development, and contract management—and sets the foundation for the delivery phase of the project. It is important to understand the services sales process—not only to sell services but to keep your company from plunging into major disasters. The process must be aligned with the customer buying behavior, flexible enough to accommodate large- and small-scale opportunities, accepted by the sales organization, and embraced by senior management

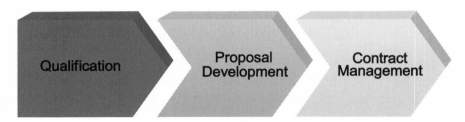

FIGURE 9.1 Professional services sales process
(See Table 9.3 for an outline of the steps in the PS sales process.)

Qualify the Opportunity

In general, service sales cycles are longer than product sales cycles. The more complex the service, the longer the sales cycle. Your sales team needs a process to sift through unqualified prospects so it can focus its time on moving qualified opportunities through the sales cycle. Prospects become motivated to work with you when you help them discover they have a problem and that you can solve their problem better than anyone else can. During the sales process, you also must build a relationship and establish credibility and trust.

Buyer vision. A consultative sales approach begins with a dialogue to understand the customer's needs. Sometimes, your sales team is fortunate enough to call on a prospect who clearly understands his company's problem and has called in your company with the expectation that your products and services can meet his needs. Other times, the buyer may be at an earlier stage in the awareness of the problem and your company's potential role in the solution. When this happens, it is up to your sales team to facilitate the awareness and linkage to your company. In *Solution Selling*, Mike Bosworth describes three levels of buyer need as follows:

1. A buyer can be at *latent pain*—unadmitted pain and no vision of solution even though the seller has a clear picture of the need and how her product or service could help the buyer. ... The two primary reasons for latent

needs are ignorance—unaware a better solution exists—or rationalization: He tried to solve the problem before and was unsuccessful.

2. If the buyer has what we call *pain*—discomfort or dissatisfaction with the current situation—he will be motivated to seek a solution if he thinks a solution is possible. ... The challenge sellers and marketers face is gaining *mindshare* of the buyer—occupying one of those foreground "slots" with an issue that their product or service can help the buyer address.

3. The third level of buyer need is *vision*—vision of a solution. ... When a buyer has latent pain or pain, the seller can create a vision for the buyer. When a buyer has an existing vision, the seller can reengineer that vision, adding the seller's aura and product or service bias to the vision.[11]

No matter the stage of your prospect, your sales team must help him formulate a clear picture of how your products and services provide the solution envisioned by him. Bosworth calls these "action visions," and his Solution Selling process provides a step-by-step system to enable your sales team to create them. Key to the approach is engineering the vision before presenting your services as the solution. You can obtain additional information about this process by reading the book *Solution Selling* or attending a Solution Selling seminar.

Information gathering.   In addition to creating the vision, your sales team will need to gather background information during the initial meeting to understand the customer's business environment. Useful information includes:

- Customer wants and needs
- History of the problem
- Scope of the problem

---

11.   Michael T. Bosworth, *Solution Selling: Creating Buyers in Difficult Selling Markets*, McGraw-Hill, 1995, pp. xxi–xxii.

- Customer commitment to the project
- Customer budget/funding for the project
- Desired timeframe to complete the project
- Whether the customer is considering assistance from other sources, either internal or external
- Buying influences and buying process
- Customer key measurement criteria
- Organizational units that are affected
- Efficiency and effectiveness of the current organizational structure
- Key individuals to be interviewed

Sales strategy. Once a project opportunity has been identified, the sales team must work together to develop a plan—a sales strategy—to win the business. The sales strategy should accomplish the following:

- Define the sales objectives
- Determine the key person responsible for the purchase decision
- Determine the key people who influence the decision
- Identify an action plan
- Determine the key people who must be involved in the sales effort
- Choose the methods that will most likely capture the contract

Qualification. Just because a prospect has communicated a problem or opportunity that you believe your company can solve, it doesn't mean that the opportunity is a good project for your company to pursue. And although this prospect may buy your hardware or software, it does not mean that the company is necessarily a good candidate for your consulting services. Qualifying prospects is an extremely important part of the professional services sales process. It protects you from wasting time and effort on unlikely prospects, impacting resource utilization if consultants are involved in the sales effort, and taking on projects that may result in losses.

TABLE 9.1 PS customer qualification checklist

- Strategy to win
- Success criteria
- Access to decision makers
- Competitive situation
- Project approach and scope
- Preliminary risk analysis
- Internal resources needed
- Third-party resources needed
- Financial plan
- Timeframe
- Proposal effort

The first qualifying step is usually after the initial meeting. At that time, a decision must be made about whether to pursue the business. The sales team typically considers the following:

- Does the customer have *funding* for the project?
- Who are the *competitors*? What are their qualifications and relationships with the customer?
- Does your company have the *resources available* with the appropriate skill set to deliver the project in a quality and timely manner?

If the answers to these basic questions reveal an opportunity worth pursuing, additional information must be gathered and reviewed to better evaluate the company and the project. Create a qualification checklist, such as the one in Table 9.1, to help you capture the important information. Assign each of the items a weight in order to calculate the probability of project success. If the project looks viable, the next step is to create a plan to win the business. By embracing a disciplined qualification process, your sales team can make the highest and best use of its time.

Management reviews. To ensure that your organization has the skill set to deliver a high-quality project and that the project will be profitable, be sure to incorporate management reviews into the sales cycle. Projects over a certain dollar amount or that present particular risk conditions should be subject to review prior to submitting a proposal. These reviews are typically conducted by a senior manager or a committee that includes senior management. If a decision is made not to bid on the project, the opportunity may be referred to a partner.

A management review process prevents projects from being overcommitted or underpriced. It educates management on the risks involved and provides strategies to minimize the risks. It also allows management to do resource planning and improve utilization rates.

Any PS organization that has ever taken on the "project from hell" knows how important it is to ensure that PS and its subcontractors are well qualified to deliver the project, and that the project makes good business sense before moving forward. When a company fails to complete a project or requires an exorbitant amount of money or resources to complete it, it learns this lesson the hard, painful way.

Manage the Proposal Process

If management determines that the project is a good business opportunity for your company, the next step is to prepare a proposal. The customer may request a proposal solely from your company or as part of a broader initiative to solicit input from a number of qualified firms.

Responding to RFPs. Your sales force may receive many Requests for Proposals (RFPs) for services. An RFP is a formal invitation to submit an offer to provide a solution to a problem or need that the customer has identified. Before responding, think carefully about the pros and cons. RFPs can consume a great deal of time by many people in your organization and show little result. In some cases the customer already has someone in mind for the project and is using the RFP to shop for price or as a tool to get the original service provider to lower its price. Don't let RFPs drain your resources. Spend enough time with the customer to ensure that you have a serious shot at the business and that you really want the business before investing time and resources in responding to an RFP.

Proposal development. To create a proposal for a large project, you need a team of people with administrative and content management skills. Oftentimes, the engagement manager or business development manager serves at the *proposal manager*. Other team members include a solution architect, relevant subject matter experts, and key subcontractors as needed. The proposal manager schedules and conducts a kickoff meeting with the team to review the win strategy, outline the proposed solution, identify and quantify overall risks and contingencies, and agree on the document process.

Work breakdown structure. A large project must be subdivided into smaller, more manageable elements. One approach is to segment the problem space and to assign a technical lead to define the technical requirements for each assigned segment. Each technical lead creates a detailed work breakdown structure (WBS) that outlines and estimates the work to be performed for the assigned solution segment. This includes the milestones, major tasks, sub-tasks, and associated deliverables. With these details in place, time and costs, pricing, and required staffing can be determined for the total solution. The detailed WBS is not included in the proposal; to do so might provide the customer with enough free information to consider doing the project in-house.

Proposal statement of work (SOW). After completing the WBS, create a functional statement of work that describes the work to be performed in general terms without providing detailed specifications. This high-level description of the solution is included with the proposal. If the proposal is accepted, the proposal SOW must be taken to the next level of detail to create the contract SOW.

Teaming agreement. If partners are required to assist in delivering a major engagement, evaluate each potential partner's interest, expertise, fees, and availability. For each selected partner, get a signed teaming agreement that the firm will provide the services at the agreed upon price if your company wins the business. You also need this pricing information to calculate the total project price for inclusion in the proposal.

A teaming agreement is a legal agreement created during the proposal phase that establishes contractual obligations between your company and the subcontractor. It identifies the relationship and division of tasks, establishes the fees for the tasks, and creates an obligation to establish a subcontractor agreement if your company is awarded the customer contract.

Financial plan. Good financial planning is essential for management to fully understand the viability of a proposal. For fixed price projects, appropriate contingency must be added to the plan to mitigate the associated risks. A financial plan includes the following items:

- Anticipated monthly and total costs (for staff, travel, included products, and any other associated expenses)
- Project price
- Payment schedule
- Revenue
- Markup
- Projected profit

Writing the proposal. An unclear, disorderly proposal doesn't garner confidence from the prospect. Plan before writing in order to avoid logic lapses and make the document as comprehensible as possible. An unresponsive proposal doesn't score points either. During planning, list all the points in the RFP that require response.

A proposal generally includes the following parts: table of contents, one-page executive summary for those who will not be reading the whole proposal (be sure to include the clincher—the approach that makes your company the only choice), introduction, main body (problem statement, project objective, benefits, approach, scope, implementation plans, deliverables, schedule, fees, assumptions), and any necessary appendices. Include success stories for similar projects to demonstrate your expertise. The proposal should be presented in a way that allows the customer to clearly discriminate between you and your competition.

Review the proposal. After all sections of the proposal are completed and assembled, be sure the proposal is adequately reviewed. It is recommended that people who have not participated in the proposal team read and critique the proposal to simulate the customer interpretation and response. Management should review and sign-off on the final proposal.

After the internal review is completed, schedule a meeting with the prospect to present the proposal. This gives your team the opportunity to emphasize key points in the strategy and approach, review the expected roles and responsibilities, confirm any assumptions, and address the customer's questions or concerns that may influence the selection process. Setting clear expectation in the proposal and meeting or exceeding those expectations during delivery is paramount to customer satisfaction.

Contract Management

In determining whether your organization is the most qualified, the customer will consider such factors as the ability of your consultants, past performance, and willingness to meet time and budget requirements. If your organization is deemed the most qualified, your sales team will meet with the customer to obtain feedback on the proposal. The final phase of the sales cycle consists of developing the contract statement of work and negotiating the final terms and conditions of the contract, including the contract fees.

TABLE 9.2 Sample contents for a contract statement of work

Component	Definition
• Objectives	A summary of the project objectives
• Project scope	The limit or boundary of the commitment
• Project approach	The methodology or logical approach to be followed
• Deliverables	The tangible results, of significant value, from the work performed
• Project organization	The roles, responsibilities, and staff requirements of the service provider and the customer teams
• Project schedule	The dates for the completion of each milestone and deliverable
• Resources	The equipment and office space required for the project
• Project controls	Project review control procedures
• Risks/Assumptions	Identified risks and assumptions that must be understood upfront and managed
• Project price	The price and payment terms for the project
• Assumptions	List of assumptions made during the planning process

Contract statement of work. Based upon the proposal and any changes or additions required by the customer, the engagement manager or project manager prepares a statement of work (see Table 9.2) with sufficient detail to manage the project scope and measure the work to be performed. Be sure to have your lead architect review the project activities, deliverables, and timeframe to ensure the integrity of the solution and schedule. It is important that the statement of work is complete and accurate to avoid any financial or legal risks. After management approves the SOW, the salesperson and engagement manager review the document with the customer manager who is authorized to approve the project. The SOW is revised and reviewed until agreement is reached.

Final contract. An in-house legal team should be assigned to your professional services organization to develop contracts, intellectual property guidelines, and other contractual documents, including a standard agreement for professional services engagements. The contract manager meets with the customer manager to discuss the terms and conditions of your standard contract and negotiate changes. The final agreement is a legal document that binds your organization to perform specific tasks and provide specific deliverables outlined in the contract statement of work, at the agreed-upon price and within the agreed-upon timeframe.

Under a fixed price contract, the customer pays your company a firm price for the work, regardless of the costs to complete the project. Whereas under a cost-reimbursable contract, the customer will reimburse your company for actual expenses incurred, up to an agreed-upon maximum. If the project expenses exceed that maximum the amount can be increased, or the project will end.

After the contract is approved, the customer submits a purchase order (another contract) for the project, and the project gets booked. Finally, the project is ready to begin. During the life of the engagement, the project manager checks that all contract terms and conditions are accommodated and obtains the customer's sign-off on the deliverables, phases, and project completion.

See Table 9.3 for an outline of the steps in the sales process.

Winning Large Deals

Unless your company's salespeople are experienced in selling complex products, they may be discouraged by the length of the sales cycle required to sell large, multifaceted services and solutions. These services frequently take a year or more to sell and a year or more to deliver.

TABLE 9.3 Typical steps in a PS sales process

Qualify the Prospect
- Identify needs that your PS organization can meet
- Help customer envision how your services provide the best solutions
- Gather information to understand the customer's business environment
- Document information listed on the qualification checklist
- Outline a sales strategy
- Conduct management review meeting

Prepare a Proposal
- Define the proposal strategy and identify a proposal team
- Outline the proposed solution
- Allocate tasks to the team
- Create the initial work breakdown structure
- Create the initial project plan
- Create third-party teaming agreements as necessary
- Create initial financial and resource plan
- Determine pricing
- Create initial risk assessment plan
- Develop the proposal and review with the team
- Conduct reviews of the proposal
- Obtain management review and sign-off
- Present proposal to prospect

Negotiate the Contract
- Obtain customer feedback on the proposal
- Develop the contract statement of work (SOW)
- Obtain management approvals
- Review SOW and pricing with customer
- Negotiate customer requests for changes
- Negotiate terms and conditions of legal agreement with customer
- Complete the final agreement, including SOW and pricing
- Obtain PS management approvals for contract/SOW
- Obtain customer approval of contract/SOW
- Request purchase order from customer
- Obtain approval on purchase order
- Establish billing schedule
- Set up project in accounting database

Large, complex services frequently provide business solutions to enterprise-wide problems. Typically, a high-level customer executive is required to sign off on a large deal. Selling at a high level requires strong relationship-building skills. Calling on managers too low in the organization is a common pitfall. Lower-level managers can become defensive if you point out what is wrong in their shop. You must reach the executives who would sleep better at night knowing that they can drive efficiencies into their business and inefficiencies out of their business by signing up for your services. Also, some complex services must be positioned across lines of business—another reason for calling high in the organization.

Get to know your customer. Understand what he does from a business perspective. Look for ways to better understand his challenges. The best approach is to do a short assessment service or workshop to discover the company's problems. You may need to provide this workshop at a discount or no charge if that is what it takes to open the door to large opportunities.

Show the customer that you truly understand his problems and discuss how you have solved similar problems for other customers. You can suggest starting with smaller services to demonstrate your value-add with quick hits. Over time, the customer will build trust in your company and your consultants. Small successes pave the path to the large deal. A customer is certainly not going to risk spending big bucks on a huge deal unless your PS organization has proved its value and earned his trust.

This approach of starting small to build trust makes sense, particularly for large, proactive solutions. In many cases, the customer doesn't see the forest for the trees. In order to get the customer's attention, you may need to start with a "band-aid" solution that merely fixes today's problem. This small service can help win the customer's respect and trust, and provide the opportunity to present the larger solution. The objective is to move the customer from a reactive mode of dealing with problems to a proactive approach that addresses the bigger picture. Proving the value-add of your consultants during small successes opens the door for you to present the vision for your larger, strategic solutions. And providing larger solutions typically opens the door to more product sales.

Even after proving your value, some companies may not be ready to sign up for a huge, expensive service. Breaking the service into phases and discussing the value provided by each phase is one way to make a large solution easier to buy. A customer who is not able to justify the funding for the huge engagement may be amenable to approving an order for the first phase or two. Breaking the project into phases also makes each phase more manageable and easier to price. And regardless of the size of the project opportunity, remember to share success stories—particularly of companies in the same industry—to prove your PS organization's competence in providing the solution.

Once the project is orally approved, it is important to get a signed contract and purchase order quickly. Be sure to begin the project in a timely manner to avoid any buyer's misgivings or changes in the organization's leadership or financial situation that may cause project delay or cancellation.

Summary

You need a well-defined sales process to successfully identify and win engagements—particularly large deals. An effective sales process guides your organization in qualifying opportunities, developing proposals, and negotiating and administering contracts.

Questions for Consideration

How effective is your sales process?

Successful consulting engagements begin with a successful sales process: prospect qualification, proposal development, and contract management. Here are some questions to consider regarding your sales process.

- Is your sales team qualified to help the customer go from buyer need to a vision of how your products and services can provide a solution to the problem?

- Which activities of the services sales cycle does your company need to improve?
  - Obtaining sales leads
  - Qualifying sales opportunities
  - Developing proposals
  - Developing contracts
  - Developing contract statements of work
  - Negotiating terms and conditions
  - Effectively involving management in the sales process

- Do account reps or product salespeople bring services salespeople or engagement managers into the account early in the sales cycle?

- Do your sales team and PS have a well-defined qualification process to ensure good business?

- Does the success rate of your proposals show a good rate of return on the time invested in proposal development?

- Do your statements of work set clear expectations upfront regarding who will do what, where, when, how, and for how much?

- Do you create teaming agreements with potential partners that define the role each will play on the project and the fees for its services?

- Do your contracts provide an adequate level of protection?

- What role does your management play in the sales cycle?

- How effective is your sales organization at winning large, complex deals that may take a year or longer to deliver?
    - Does your sales team call on managers at the appropriate level in the organization?
    - Does your sales team follow a strategic approach, using assessments and small services successes to lead to bigger services wins?
    - Does your sales team work effectively with PS engagement managers in order to break large engagements into smaller phases in order to get customer sign-off?

10

Productize for Easier Entrée, Sale, and Delivery

Packaging services—with a fixed price, defined scope, methodology, deliverables, and timetable—can make services easier to sell and deliver, while reducing project risk.

The knowledge and confidence displayed by salespeople within the well-defined parameters of products often disappear when they enter the fuzzy world of custom services. Instead of pitching products based on concrete specs, functions, and pricing, sellers are faced with having to understand customers' problems, describing alternative solutions, and helping select the best approach. And often salespeople need to forge this new path to sales without any formal training. It is no wonder that product salespeople are often unmotivated or unsuccessful in the foreign environment of custom services.

Product salespeople are trained and experienced in selling products and comfortable presenting them to prospects. They understand the usual phases of a product sale. They know how to leverage sales and marketing materials, how to make the most of customer references, when to bring in an executive, and the kinds of problems customers are trying to solve with their products. What better way to help *product* salespeople sell services than to make the services resemble *products*?

With a packaged—or what is often called a "productized"—service, the sales force can fully and in a well-ordered way talk about services. They know the activities or tasks performed by the consultants, as well as the deliverables—because they're predefined. The price, timeframe, and the approach used to deliver the service are delineated as part of the package. Making the services sale concrete creates a familiarity that the sale force can deal with.

With a productized service, not only does the sales force feel more comfortable selling services using its proven sales techniques for products, but also consultants find the services easier to deliver using a predefined process.

On the surface, productizing services looks like an ideal solution for product-centric companies to manage the challenges presented by the intangible nature of services. Although packaging services has its benefits, it is not a panacea for a company's services sales shortfalls. As in any business investment, the return must outweigh the costs. In this chapter, we will look at the pros and cons of packaging services, criteria for selecting the best services to package, and a "product development process" for services.

Who Benefits from Packaged Services?

Packaged services can bridge the gap between tangible products and invisible services by adding concrete elements—specific activities and deliverables, limited time period, definite price tag—to the services picture. Let's look at the many ways sales reps, marketing managers, consultants, professional services organizations, partners, and customers benefit from packaged services.

Sales representatives

- Identify the target market and the business or technical issues addressed by the service
- Describe service activities and deliverables

- Capture new customers or new markets with a more compelling value proposition
- Tell the customer how long the service will take and how much it will cost
- Share results achieved by other customers who purchased the same service

Marketing managers

- Use product marketing techniques to promote the service
- Give the service a simple descriptive name and announce it in a press release
- Include the service on a price list
- Create sales guides, service briefs, Web-based descriptions, and presentations as sales tools
- Capture customer success stories to share with customers desiring the same service

Consultants

- Deliver service using a standard process (methodology)
- Require less time to prepare for delivery of a service project
- Leverage sample deliverables and templates, such as a report or a questionnaire
- Learn to perform the service in a consistent manner
- Capture tips and techniques from each service delivery to assist other consultants
- Speed the sales and delivery processes by standardizing the statement of work, project plan, and other project management tools for service
- Include options that empower the customer to gain the best-fit solution

PS organization

- Make service easily repeatable
- Employ less experienced consultants to deliver service
- Ensure consistent and efficient service delivery with higher quality across multiple locations
- More accurately predict resourcing needs and improve utilization
- Deliver service at a lower cost
- Price service to ensure desired profits by calculating the delivery time and level of resources
- Achieve higher margins

Partners

- More easily sell service using a clear description, fixed price, and supporting marketing materials
- More expertly deliver service using a well-documented methodology and tools

Customers

- Know upfront how much a service will cost and how long it will take
- Don't have to worry about cost overruns or getting an unexpected result
- Receive a written description of the service and success stories about other customers who purchased the service
- Benefit from the accumulated knowledge consultants gain from performing the same service for many customers
- Feel confident that the results will be similar to those gained by other customers in the past

With so many benefits from packaging services, product companies often jump into productizing services without understanding the limitations, how to select appropriate services to package, and how to implement packaging effectively.

It's Not a Panacea

For product-centric companies, productizing services may appear to be the natural thing to do—it's in the company's DNA. Everyone knows that *product* is one of the four P's of marketing. You obviously must build a product before you sell it, but you don't have to package a consulting service to sell one.

One client, who had recently made the transition from product marketing to services marketing, read a book about productizing services. Then he proceeded to package a service and launch it in the same way he had introduced products for the company. After completing the launch, the service didn't sell. He then tasked the telemarketing group to call prospects in the market sector. This only produced a few leads. By the time I met him he realized that following the same approach he used as a product marketing manager was not going to work for services.

Packaged services have their place, but they are not the remedy for all the challenges faced in marketing and selling professional services. In fact, there is an inherent danger in reinforcing a *product* sales and marketing model for services—it can deter salespeople from making the transition to *solution selling*. As discussed earlier in this book, solution selling takes a different approach to sales. The salesperson must have a firm grasp on his customer's business, build a careful connection between the customer's specific business issues and his company's services, and present them in such a manner that the customer believes his unique needs will be met. The company and product pitches are replaced with tools that assist the sales rep in structuring a consultative, diagnostic conversation with the customer to develop a deep understanding of the issues or opportunities. There are important skills here that salespeople need to develop.

As with any business decision, before you make a commitment to packaged services, make sure you are clear about what you hope to gain from the effort and do sufficient upfront homework to select services that justify the investment.

Packaging services takes time and money. It requires participation from the marketing and methodology groups to develop services, as well as training for consultants and salespeople. As with any development effort, you want to feel confident that you will produce enough revenue to recoup the costs and make a profit. Let's take a look at some of the shortcomings of packaged services from several viewpoints.

Customer perspective. Would you rather pick a home from a few models or have one custom-designed to your specifications? The answer is clear—if a buyer is going to spend a great deal of money on something that is of great importance, he would prefer to present his requirements, be involved in the design, and have a solution designed to meet his needs. A customer also expects to spend more money on something that is custom designed to match his needs, than an off-the-shelf product. However, the smaller the purchase, the less interest the buyer has in devoting time or money to a customized solution. If the buyer wants a new window for a house, he will more likely choose among standard windows than invest the time in having one built to his specifications.

The same is true for consulting projects. Many customers value custom services more than packaged services. But the smaller and more standardized the project, the more likely the customer will be happy with packaged services. If a customer needs to migrate from one release of an operating system to another, a standard service offering likely will serve this need. For major projects, a customer will want the service customized to his own needs—or at least believe that it is being custom designed.

Sales perspective. In the product world, much upfront work is done before a product is ready to sell. Before committing to build a product, companies conduct sufficient research to evaluate the size of the market and the competition. Before mass-producing a product, beta tests are held with several customers. The success stories and references from the initial customer experiences strengthen the marketing story as well as the product. Confident in the product and its markets, companies invest in marketing programs and sales training to launch the product and sell it to a larger audience.

A similar approach must be applied to services. Start by presenting your services ideas to a few customers in your target market. Deliver the services and capture the success stories and references. Use these customer references to attract more customers. Once you get to the point where you know that there is a large market for this service, packaging the service may make it easier to sell and deliver to a large audience. Even if you plan to use third-party sales channels to sell your packaged services, you still must ensure that there is a large enough market to warrant the expense of packaging services and training the sales channel.

Delivery perspective. Would you buy expensive machinery and build a large factory to make a product before you were sure there was a real market and you could sell it in large quantities? No— you would probably build a few prototypes by hand and refine the product based on customer feedback. By doing so, you can change the product to meet the unique needs of each customer and avoid high manufacturing costs until you learn more about the market requirements. You may continue to proceed in this fashion, until the market demand becomes so large that you need to create economies of scale. You may then decide to build a factory so you can mass produce the product. By utilizing standard processes, you reduce your costs and increase your revenues.

Likewise, there is no reason to invest in fully documented methodology and training for a service if you do not know whether there is considerable market demand for it. Start by using well-qualified consultants to deliver the services to the initial customers. When the demand for the service outstrips your resources to deliver it, it is time to ask yourself whether hiring or training a few more well-qualified consultants is the solution—or if the demand for the specific service is large enough to justify the investment in developing and documenting a specific methodology with supporting marketing materials. In that way, less experienced consultants can be trained to effectively deliver the service and product salespeople can more easily sell it.

There are many other ways to leverage your delivery resources beyond creating methodology for packaged services. Provide additional training for your consultants in the specific related competency, develop methodology or tools for service modules that are performed frequently (such as a questionnaire to conduct an assessment), or invest in capturing and sharing the knowledge gained from similar consulting projects. Be sure you have clearly defined your needs and objectives so you can choose the best way of using your delivery resources.

The big picture. Packaged services have their place, but they can also end up being a huge drain of time, money, and people resources. So be sure you are clear about your reasons for packaging a service. Ask yourself if there may be another solution that can better meet your objectives. If you decide that packaging services is the best solution, be sure to prioritize all your ideas for services packaging to ensure that you are using your resources in the best possible way.

Choosing Services to Package

Once you have made a decision to invest in packaging services, the next question is: Which services should you package? Services marketing managers need to take a close look at how well a productized offering will meet the needs of their customers before packaging a service.

TABLE 10.1 Questions to consider before packaging a service

- What is the service and who will it be sold to?
- How large is the market?
- How many times have you delivered a similar service?
- What is the value to the sales organization in packaging this service?
- What is the value to the delivery organization in packaging this service?
- Are there more efficient or economical ways to meet the needs of the sales and delivery organizations?
- Are consultants who have delivered the service in the past available to assist with the methodology development effort and training?
- How many customers do you expect to sell this service to in the next year? Two years? Five years?
- How many times must you deliver this service in order to recoup the projected development costs?
- What is the projected revenue and profit from this service?

Your packaged services must be well targeted and well defined to be successful door openers and revenue generators.

Package the winners. One of the best ways to select services to package is to choose similar ones that are already being successfully sold and delivered by your PS practices. Your consulting practice in Paris may be experiencing great success in selling and delivering a particular service to a large number of its customers. This same service could be a winner in other locations throughout the world. If there is a clear market for a particular service, providing marketing materials and service delivery methodology will make it easier to sell and deliver.

Assessment services. You need a way to understand a customer's business challenges—the areas where they need the most assistance. Customers need a way to evaluate your expertise and your ability to add value to their organization at a low cost before they commit to a larger project. One of the best ways to meet both of these needs is with a service that evaluates the strengths and weaknesses of some aspect of the customer's technical or business environment, such as a security assessment service or a network assessment service. It allows the customer to evaluate the expertise you bring to the table, while containing the time, money, and effort invested in the initial consulting engagement with your company. This type of service is often priced at a low fee to help get your foot in the door and provide a better understanding of the areas where your service offerings can add value to the customer.

Packaging the assessment service makes it easier to sell and deliver. A sales rep can boast to a new prospect: "In five days, our security experts can assess your security strategy, identify the strengths and weaknesses of your current approach, and evaluate the risks to your IT infrastructure and business data. You will receive a report with the results of the evaluation as well as a presentation of the results. The cost is $10,000." Using a packaged service—that identifies a timeframe, activities, deliverables, and costs—the salesperson can present the service offering with minimal involvement from the PS organization.

Product jumpstart services. Another good service to package is one that enables customers to get up-to-speed quickly in the use of a product after purchase. A packaged service that includes product installation, optimization, planning, and training on best practices may enable customers to jumpstart projects. This type of service can be easily sold at the same time as the product, provides immediate value at a reasonable price, and opens the door for follow-on consulting engagements.

Managing the Packaged Services Process

To streamline your packaging efforts, use a standardized process to go from service selection to service launch. Using your company's standard hardware or software process to package services doesn't work. The process must be designed specifically for packaging consulting services.

Packaging services requires cross-functional teams to work together towards a common goal. Assign a marketing person to project manage the entire process. The most common approach for bringing new products or services to market includes stages and gates. The gates serve as the quality control checkpoints at which management decides whether or not to continue the project development. To implement this approach, you need gatekeepers or decision makers to make the go/kill decision at each gate. The gatekeepers for the early stages may be different than the ones for the final stages. For the final stage gatekeepers, consider including the leaders (or designees) of the following groups: PS organization, PS practices, training, marketing, and service methodology. Gatekeepers must be empowered to make decisions and not be afraid to cancel projects.

Following is a suggested process for packaging services that is similar—but not the same—as a new product introduction process:

Stage 1: Idea selection. Determine what you want to accomplish— drive more product sales, simplify service sales, reduce the cost of service delivery, improve service quality and consistency, reach a wider market. Then select services that will best achieve your goals.

Idea generation. Winning service ideas are based on real customer needs and actual service delivery experience. Suggestions for packaged services must come from practice managers, consultants, and salespeople who are engaging with customers on a daily basis—not a corporate organization that has little exposure to customers.

To facilitate the flow of ideas from the right sources, establish a formal process for the submission and evaluation of ideas. Develop a convenient submission form. Assign an individual—usually someone in the marketing organization—to be the focal point for receiving new ideas, for having them evaluated, and for responding to the originator. Provide written feedback in a timely manner so that submitters feel they have been heard and their ideas are truly being considered.

Concept evaluation. For service ideas that merit further consideration, assign someone—the focal person mentioned above or the appropriate marketing manager—to conduct a quick, high-level analysis. In a few pages, document the concept for the review committee. Include the service description, objectives, and target market, as well as estimated resources, skills, and start-up costs.

Gate: Concept review. To ensure that each service is being fairly appraised, develop a list of evaluation criteria, such as market potential, development cost, incremental company profits, differentiation potential, time for payback, resource availability, partner access— with an assigned weight for each. Calculate the total score for each service and compare it against other proposed services.

Stage 2: Service requirements (business case). When a service concept is approved, assign a marketing manager to provide a more in-depth analysis. This is similar to a product requirements document in a classical product development process

Service requirements document. Include the following:
- Describe the service (including the problem the service solves; service activities; and deliverables, such as presentations, reports, etc.)
- Describe the market and the competition
- Describe the service benefits
- Define the strategies for pricing, promoting, selling, and delivering the service
- Outline the process to deliver the service
- Determine the resource requirements to develop the packaged service methodology and tools
- Estimate skills and resources to sell and deliver the service
- Prepare a business case with the projected price, sales, costs, revenues, and profits

Gate: Service requirements review. During this review meeting, the gatekeepers decide whether to invest in packaging the service. If the project gets the green light, resources must be assigned to develop and execute the service plans.

Stage 3: Service plans and development. The assigned personnel develop the service plans for delivery methodology, sales and delivery training, and marketing; and execute the plans.

Methodology plan. If a company decides to invest in packaged services, typically a services engineering organization is created with responsibility for methodology. This group prepares a plan for the packaged service methodology and tools, including the service project plans, technical deliverables, people and skills required for delivery, partner requirements, risk factors, schedules, and costs. Services cannot be developed in an "ivory tower." It is crucial to get experienced consultants involved in the development process.

Training plan. The education organization defines a plan that covers the required training needed to deliver the service, how and when the courses will be developed, who will deliver them, the number of consultants requiring training in each geography, a proposed training schedule, and the associated costs. If sales training is needed, similar plans need to be defined.

Marketing plan. Marketing puts together a plan that unites all organizations within a company to work toward a single goal—to make prospects want to do business with you and purchase the service. The marketing plan exploits your company's strengths, neutralizes perceived weaknesses, identifies customer opportunities, crystallizes your offerings, articulates the customer benefits, and sizes up the competition. The plan defines the customer deliverables (service briefs, success stories), promotion (websites, conference calls, press releases, and analyst briefings), and sales tools (sales guides, presentations) for the new packaged service.

Service development. Once the methodology, training, and marketing, plans are completed and approved, the next step is to execute the plans and produce the deliverables. Holding team meetings with all the players (marketing, education, methodology) participating in the development process helps monitor the progress, keep the development on schedule, and facilitate the discussion and resolution of issues.

Gate: Plans and deliverables review. All plans and deliverables must be reviewed to ensure they are completed in a satisfactory manner. For the review to be effective, you must identify the people with the appropriate skills to evaluate the plans and conduct a thorough examination of the deliverables.

Stage 4: Testing and readiness evaluation. Before launching the service, validate the service methodology and its repeatability with real customers. Also ensure that resources are available and trained to sell and deliver the service in all planned geographies.

Beta test. A service beta test is similar to a product beta test. Testing the service early on at several customer sites before generally offering the service validates the methodology, ensures that consultants can easily follow the methodology, and confirms the timeframe and resources needed for each phase of the service. Beta tests also provide the opportunity to evaluate proposals, customer presentations, and other sales materials. Because the service preparation is even more elaborate for a packaged service than a custom service, no price concessions should be necessary for beta test customers. In fact, there is no reason to tell the customer that the service delivery is a beta test of a packaged service. The main objectives of the beta test is to ensure that consultants can use the methods and tools to deliver the service in the defined timeframe, and to capture success stories to assist with future sales.

Gate: Service readiness review. Just as all aspects of a product are reviewed to determine its readiness to be sold and delivered, a readiness plan and review is recommended for a packaged service. It is critical that the review include all the items outlined above *plus* the readiness of the field organization. Are salespeople and consultants trained on the service? In other words, can salespeople identify and qualify prospects, describe the service, and answer questions? Are the marketing materials localized and translated? Materials might include anything from a service brief to a success story. Are local price lists updated to include the service? The gatekeepers must check that everything is in place, including the launch plans.

Stage 5: Service launch. After three or more successful beta tests and approval from your service readiness review team, you are ready to launch the new packaged service as defined in the go-to-market plans for your new packaged service. Be sure to tout your customer successes in all your launch materials and events. After all your hard work, your sales team will feel empowered to successfully sell your new service and skilled consultants will be available to deliver the service with high quality and within the defined timeframe.

Step 6: Continuous improvement. To achieve the highest possible quality and margins with the least possible effort, be sure to gather input from delivery consultants, sales team, and customers. Incorporate the recommendations to improve each packaged service and evaluate the overall packaging program.

Enhance packaged services. Just as a product needs new releases and new marketing plans after it is released, a service also must be evaluated after it is released. Methodology must be enhanced over time to incorporate the lessons learned from the delivery experiences. And just as a product outlives its usefulness over time, a packaged service's life must be ended when it no longer meets the needs of the market.

Measure value of packaging program. In order to win the opportunity to continue to package services, there must be a way to measure their value. Comparing the revenue generated from a packaged service with the cost for the development effort provides a measurement

TABLE 10.2 Professional service packaging process

1. Idea selection

2. Service requirements (business case)

3. Service plans and development

4. Testing and readiness evaluation

5. Service launch

6. Continuous improvement

for management to evaluate the value of packaging. Of course, this requires tracking the resources and time investments for development, as well as the number of packaged services sold.

The services packaging process is usually less rigorous than a product development process. Companies often miss the mark either by not having any real process in place to develop methodology, tools, training, and marketing materials, or—at the other extreme—by using a process that is more time consuming and tedious than is necessary to accomplish the goals. Periodically review your reasons for packaging services and refine your process to meet your objectives.

Bundling Services with Products

Prior to 1969, almost all training, support, and professional services were bundled with hardware products. In fact, most software was also bundled. The customer paid for the hardware and everything else was "free." And, of course, the margins on hardware were huge. Ah, those were the days!

Over many decades, customers have finally accepted that software, consulting, support, and training have their own unique value—and their own price tag. However, in the quest to facilitate sales of

TABLE 10.3 Sample marketing materials and delivery methodology
components for packaged services

Marketing Materials

- Statement of work
- Press release
- Service brief
- Sales guide
- Presentation slides
- Success stories
- Fixed price

Delivery Methodology

- Repeatable methodology
- Roles and activities
- Timetable for service delivery
- Templates/reusable content
- Questionnaires
- Sample reports
- Automation tools
- End-user training materials

professional services, some companies bundle the service with the
product. There are several points that should be seriously considered
before taking this step.

Services demand respect as value add. If your company is serious
about being in the services business, you must establish services as
a fee-based function versus hoping to recoup the costs with product
margins. By bundling services with products, customers may view
the services as free. To successfully charge for services, be sure you
communicate the benefits to customers, such as productivity gains,
labor savings, ergonomic improvements, or faster time to market.

People value what they pay for. It is human nature, to place more value on services that require a fee than services that are perceived to be free. In cases where a service was provided at no extra charge, I have seen customers go about their busy day and let consultants sit around for hours—wasting their time—before making the time to meet with them or provide them with required data. When the service is paid for separately, the customer commits to the roles and responsibilities as outlined in the statement of work and respects the consultants' time—particularly if the service is being billed as T&M (time and materials).

Summary

Packaging services makes services easier to market and sell, substantially reduces implementation time and costs, delivers higher quality through consistency and repeatability, and diminishes risks for the customer. However, although packaging services has its benefits, it is not a panacea for a company's services sales shortfalls. Be sure to carefully choose which services to package, use an effective service development process, track sales, and measure the return on your investment.

Questions for Consideration

Does your company understand how to package services?

Salespeople in product companies are usually not trained to sell consulting services. A common solution is to package services like products so that they are easier to sell. It is important to understand the pros and cons of packaged services, how to select services for packaging, and how to package services. Here are some topics for consideration to evaluate your company's effectiveness in packaged services.

- What are the benefits of your packaged services?
  - For your sales force
  - For your marketing organization
  - For your consultants
  - For your partners
  - For your customers

- How do you choose services to package?
  - Who is involved in the selection process? Is there adequate involvement from the consulting practices?
  - What research is done to evaluate the market for a packaged service before beginning the development effort?
  - What criteria are used for evaluating services to package?
  - How would you rate the services your company selected for packaging to date? What services are the most profitable? Least profitable? Most effective? Least effective?

- What methods do you use to package services?
  - Is a business case developed and approved by management?
  - Are adequate resources assigned?
  - Are plans developed for the marketing, methodology, and training materials?

- o   Are the top subject matter experts included on the methodology development team?
- o   Is someone assigned to track the progress of the packaging effort?
- o   Are review meetings held on a regular basis?
- o   Is each service tested with several customers before it is marketed on a wide basis?
- o   Is the readiness of the field organization (i.e., sales, delivery resources, local marketing) considered before launching a service on a global basis?
- o   Is feedback solicited from customers?
- o   Are your services enhanced based on the feedback from customers, sales, and delivery experiences?

- How do you rate your company's process for packaging services?
  - o   Is the process customized specifically for packaged consulting services? Or does you company utilize the same process used for product development?
  - o   Do the results justify the effort expended? Is the process too rigorous or not structured enough?

- How do you measure your investments in packaged services?
  - o   Do you have a method for tracking sales of packaged sales and the resulting revenue?
  - o   If a packaged service is customized during delivery, is it counted in the tracking of packaged services engagements?
  - o   Do the services revenues from your packaged services justify the time and resource expense of the packaging efforts?

- Are packaged services the best solution to accomplish your objectives?
  - o   Would more effective marketing materials and reference accounts for *custom* services meet your objectives?
  - o   Do your salespeople require more training to sell *custom* services?

- o   Is a greater investment needed to capture and share among your consultants the intellectual property (knowledge, ideas) gained from the delivery of *custom* services?
- o   Is service delivery methodology or project management methodology needed to assist in delivering *custom* services (discussed in next chapter)?
- o   Do your consultants need more training on products, technologies, or industries?

11

Optimize Services Delivery

Every professional services organization must invest in its consultants—its chief assets—and its methods to ensure efficient, consistent, and quality engagements.

Customers want *solutions* to solve their technology and business challenges and build competitive advantage. A PS organization delivers these solutions to customers through its *people*, *processes*, and *technology*. High-quality solutions result in *references* from customers, and this leads to *additional business* opportunities. A simple way to view the business is to use the following formula:

People + Process + Technology =

Quality Solutions → References → Additional Business

People are your organization's most important strategic assets. Their expertise and practical, hands-on experience enable them to understand customer needs and deliver innovative solutions. Documented methods, proven to produce quality results, accelerate the solution implementation and ensure the functional and technical success of each solution. Tools and technology significantly enhance productivity and enable consistent results.

To build a solid foundation for delivering quality solutions, professional services organizations must:

- Recruit and hire the best people
- Invest in training to build consultant skills
- Motivate consultants to perform at their best
- Share the knowledge and lessons learned with all consultants
- Provide methodology and tools to leverage consultant time and talents

In this chapter, we will explore each of these success factors.

Choose the Right Talent

Professional services is a people-intensive business. Attracting and hiring the best possible people to deliver your services is key to business success. Each person contributes to one side or the other of the balance sheet: good performers are assets who generate income; poor performers are liabilities who result in losses. A star performer is in demand by customers, contributes to the organization's reputation, and helps capture positive references. A person who lacks the skill set to deliver your services will find himself spending a good deal of time on the bench and negatively impacting your utilization rate. You want all your consultants active and productive. And, as important as possessing technical skills, you want consultants with interpersonal skills that make them welcome contributors in the customer environment. Lack of interpersonal skills can contribute to no follow-up engagements and negative references.

New hires can become better performers with the right tools and training. However, starting with the right characteristics hastens employee development. To hire the best talent, first you must gain clarity on the base-level skills you require. Do this by developing a clear profile for each type of position in your organization. Interviewing your current top performers will enable you to identify the desired characteristics to include in a job profile.

TABLE 11.1 Important interpersonal skills and attitudes
             for consultants

- Integrity
- Concern for customer business issues
- Enthusiasm for technology and the solution
- Attitude that goes the extra mile
- Good written and oral skills (a communicator)
- Group reliance and cooperation skills (a team player)

Using these job profiles as guides, select candidates who not only have the right technical or project management skills for the position, but also the interpersonal skills and attitudes to interact effectively with customers. (See Table 11.1 for a list of some of the key characteristics.) Next have several people in your organization interview the candidates to make sure that they are suitable for the position and your group. You may need to interview the finalists several times to make sure they are a good match.

Being a consultant usually involves extensive travel, long work hours, and interaction with new people on every engagement. Be sure that the demands of the job and the work environment are clearly understood during the interviewing phase. Individuals who relish change and challenge and enjoy working with people do well in a consulting role.

Match people and roles. PS organizations attract smart professionals with a high need for achievement. Generally, consultants get bored easily and hate doing repetitive work. Professionals like the challenge of new projects and assignments that stretch their skills. Yet, not every job requires the most skilled talent. If a consulting group has too many senior people, higher-priced people end up performing lower-value tasks where they are overqualified. Matching the level of the consultant to the skill requirements of the job is important to maintain employee morale, as well as to maximize profits.

Match supply with demand. Then there is the ongoing issue of managing the supply/demand consultant balance. Unfortunately, the availability of top talent and the availability of engagements are often inversely related. When the economy is running at full steam, such as during the "dot-com" era, engagements are easy to come by but experienced consultants are scarce. PS management must work harder to attract the best talent, and recruit an adequate number of consultants to meet the demand at a salary that allows the business to still make a profit. At times like this, other incentives besides salary help to recruit talented people. In contrast, when the economy and the business environment are stalled, consultants are plentiful but consulting sales slow considerably. This occurred in the early 2000 years after the dot-com bubble burst and again in 2008 and 2009. In this kind of environment, engagements are harder to come by, and staff reduction may be necessary. To manage the ebb and flow of projects, consider utilizing your network of subcontractors to create a scalable business during both prosperous and challenging times.

Develop and Retain Star Performers

Once consultants are hired, the task becomes how to get the maximum value from them and retain the top performers. This requires investing in training, making sure consultants are being assigned to projects where they can learn and grow, and providing career opportunities for growth.

Training. When consultants are hired, it takes time for them to get up to speed. They need to attend training programs to understand the company environment, management team, processes and procedures, methodologies, tools, and other unique aspects of the company. Because every organization has its own unique methods and products, training is required even if a consultant brings a great deal of experience to the job. In addition, technical consultants and engagement managers must continue to receive training *every year* in order to remain current in their specialized area of expertise.

Mentoring. In addition to formal classroom training, PS organizations must invest in on-the-job training and mentoring. The natural tendency of management is to assign consultants to projects similar to ones they have done before to ensure quality work and customer satisfaction. Yet, managers also need to consider developing the skills of their consultants when they assign projects. Junior people must be matched with more senior people so they can observe a skilled person performing an activity and learn from the experience. And senior people need to mentor junior people to monitor their performance when doing a new task for the first time or two. Besides benefit to the person being mentored, the mentor himself experiences a purposefulness that can be rejuvenating.

Retaining top talent. Once consultants are hired and trained, retaining the best performers is crucial. Understanding why star employees leave is the first step in creating a strategy to retain them. Track your employee turnover rate and include a breakdown by performance levels. Notice if turnover is greater in particular performance levels, job categories, solution practices, or locations.

Top performers like to take pride in their own work and their company. Organizations that embody excellence are far more likely to attract and retain the best of the best. By setting the standards high and managing out poor performers, you can create an environment where quality is delivered every time.

Providing consultants with mentoring, interesting and challenging engagements, development opportunities, competitive salaries, and fair treatment will help to kindle satisfaction and commitment. Rotate professionals among various functional areas to keep them motivated and engaged. And be sure to recognize team performance, not just star performance. Showing genuine appreciation is one of the strongest motivators.

Motivate and Cultivate Teamwork

Professional services is a project-based business. Success strongly depends on teams of people combining their efforts effectively to create set deliverables within a set schedule. While working on projects, consultants often spend a good deal of their time at customer facilities. Once a project is completed, the team is disbanded and the players join new engagement teams. This structure results in pockets of knowledge and tools. To overcome this weakness inherent in a project-based business, management needs to foster strong communication and collaboration in the organization. Here are a few of the ways managers can achieve these results.

Communicate vision and goals. Top management in PS organizations focuses a great deal of time on talking to prospective customers, qualifying opportunities, negotiating contracts, ensuring projects are running on time and on budget, and interfacing with corporate executives. So much time is consumed running the day-to-day operations that there is often little time devoted to the most important task of providing direction on where the PS organization is going.

Because consultants are working on engagements, removed from management and peers, it becomes even more important to ensure that consultants have a sense of the bigger, corporate purpose and how their contributions play an important role. Leaders must articulate the organization's vision, as well as the corporation's vision—and show how they interrelate—not only for the health of the business but also for the sake of consultants. Besides establishing a clear direction, managers must win commitment from everyone on the team to support the vision. Without a strong sense of vision and teamwork, a consultant may feel more connected with his customer's organization than his own.

Foster knowledge sharing. Professionals working in the same functional competency or the same industry need to meet to share their knowledge. Classes and workshops provide the opportunity for consultants to meet and interact with people from other offices in the company. Besides fostering knowledge transfer, these meetings promote teamwork and cooperation among individuals across geographies.

Annual or semiannual meetings of the entire PS organization are a terrific way to bring people together from all geographic practices. Practice managers, engagement managers, project managers, and consultants have the opportunity to meet and spend some quality time with their counterparts throughout the world. A person is much more likely to contact a peer to exchange ideas after he has met with his counterpart face to face.

In addition to formal training and organization-wide meetings, other means of sharing information—such as discussion groups, online chat groups, and summit meetings—should be established on an ongoing basis for each competency area. And be sure to schedule social events to drive camaraderie.

Create space for success. While fostering collaboration, you also need to respect individuals by giving them the freedom to make a difference. You hire specialists who are experts in their field. They typically work at customer locations independently of management. When challenges occur, they need to make intelligent decisions quickly. Micromanagement doesn't work. Here is some excellent advice on managing and motivating consultants from David Maister's book *Managing the Professional Services Firm.*

> In the management of professionals the supervisor should be very clear on the *what* ('provide clear goals'), spend only the bare minimum of time on the *how* ('involve them in decision making,' 'provide autonomy') and spend a lot of time on the *why* ('provide meaning').[12]

---

12. David H. Maister, *Managing the Professional Service Firm*, New York, NY: The Free Press, 1993, p. 171.

Implement a Skills Database

In the product business, supplier relations are managed and multiple suppliers are identified as sources for all product parts. Parts are tracked and restocked as necessary. Many companies implement supply-chain extranets to connect with their supply-chain partners. These extranets typically enable companies to reduce costs, improve procurement-and-supply decisions, and respond quickly to product quality issues. In short, supply-chain management is understood, valued, and effectively handled by most product companies.

In the services business, experts with the particular skills needed to deliver a project are the "product parts." Unfortunately, they cannot be cloned and put on a shelf until needed. Locating the subject matter experts when you need them, where you need them, and at a price you are willing to pay are challenging facets of managing engagement resources. Some of the talent may be in other locations within your company; some available from partners with whom you have worked; and some still to be located from other sources. Maintaining a comprehensive skills database is crucial to locate experts and effectively manage resource utilization.

A skills database is a repository that provides the name of all subject-matter experts within your organization as well as those available from partners. You can build your own skills database or purchase one. The database often includes the following details about each consultant:

- Skill sets and levels of competency
- Details of expertise
- Location
- Languages spoken
- Industry experience
- Prior work performed for your organization
- Performance ratings and comments on prior projects

To be effective, the database must be maintained by adding new consultants and subcontractors, new skills and industry experience developed by individuals, and performance information relating to completed projects. Database reports can identify skills, gaps, and trends. When properly maintained, a skills database is an invaluable tool to quickly find the right consultant for the job and maximize your resource utilization.

Develop Project Management Methodology

Every professional services organization needs a project management methodology so engagement managers and project managers can consistently plan and manage engagements successfully. The project management methodology should encompass *all* aspects of a project from project initiation through project closure. This includes specific processes for project planning, status reporting, change management, issue management, quality management, risk management, and more. Methodology models frequently include processes, procedures, best practices, workflows, checklists, questionnaires, worksheets, and examples. Table 11.2 provides a list of typical activities for managing and closing an engagement. The sales process (qualification, proposal, contract management) was covered in Chapter 9. It is important that the sales process and project management methodology are well documented, understood, maintained, and appropriately disseminated.

Some of the benefits of a standard project management methodology follow:

- Provides consistency and quality throughout the business operations
- Minimizes business risk
- Enhances delivery of high-quality services
- Improves cost-effectiveness of consulting assignments
- Establishes a common language for the organization
- Improves communications within the organization
- Enables mobility of resources across projects and geographies
- Facilitates training of new project managers

A product company would not hire individuals in manufacturing and let each one determine how best to build the product in his own way. Likewise, services organizations need methods or best practices to ensure that quality services are delivered on time and on budget.

Experienced consultants, trained by many different companies, have their own way of managing and implementing projects. Trying to get people who have been doing things one way for many years to change their practices can be challenging. Yet methods to drive quality results consistently are critical—particularly when engagements are performed at customer locations away from management. And, of course, professionals who have not worked in a prior consulting role have even a greater need for direction.

It is highly recommended that managers or designated appointees from each geographical region—North America, South America, Europe, Asia Pacific—be involved in developing and reviewing the project management methodology. This ensures the methodology is applicable to all regions and that there is buy-in of all practice managers. To be successful, every manager must enforce the use of the methodology in his practice.

Invest in Service Delivery Methodology

In addition to a project management methodology, professional services organizations can benefit from service delivery methods. The project management methodology provides a framework for managing *all* engagements (e.g., project planning, status reporting, issue management), whereas service delivery methodology provides methods, tools, and templates to aid consultants in delivering *specific* services (e.g., security assessment, storage consolidation, disaster recovery, IT infrastructure optimization).

Although services are usually customized for each customer, there is often a fair amount of similarity in solutions for a particular market segment—thus allowing the possible formation of a methodology. By investing in these methodologies, PS organizations enable consultants to deliver services more efficiently and with consistently higher quality.

The level of detail in a methodology can vary considerably depending upon the type of service and your objectives. For example, a service to install or configure a product may have a very detailed process that describes the steps in "cook-book" fashion so the service can easily and quickly be delivered by junior consultants. Whereas, a methodology to develop a Web-based architecture for an ecommerce environment accommodating millions of users, cannot be as tightly structured. And even with the methodology, it may require senior consultants with extensive training and experience to deliver the service.

Packaged service methodology. A packaged service provides a quality solution with a fixed set of activities and deliverables, a defined number of consultants and their skills, and a fixed timeframe. With this information, service providers can determine the cost to deliver the service and set a fixed fee to meet profit goals.

The methodology generally includes the following:

- Statement of work
- Project plan with time allotted for each phase
- Technical approach
- Process to perform service activities
- Tools to speed the delivery process
- Report templates and sample reports
- Risk factors and plans to manage the risks

In some cases, the activities and deliverables of a service remain somewhat constant but the timeframe varies for each engagement by the number of servers, storage devices, or other factors. Although the time and cost of the service varies, it is still possible to define processes and sample deliverables to enable consultants to deliver the service with consistent quality.

Service components methodology. Even if your organization mainly delivers custom services, there is still a level of commonality

TABLE 11.2 Typical activities for managing PS engagements

Start-up

- Complete detailed project plan
- Update financial plan, risk assessment
- Obtain subcontractor agreements
- Conduct internal kickoff meeting
- Conduct customer kickoff meeting
- Obtain customer approval on project plan

Ongoing Project Management

- Update project plan, SOW, financial plan, risk assessment throughout the project
- Track project status with progress reviews and progress reports
- Track project quality with technical reviews and quality reviews/audits
- Manage issues and changes in scope
- Manage time/expense reporting and subcontractor payment
- Manage revenue milestones and customer billing

Solution Delivery

- Collect information necessary to deliver the service
- Coach customer staff/conduct formal training
- Develop solution components
- Plan delivery of solution components
- Prepare acceptance package
- Test solution
- Obtain customer's approval on deliverables
- Deliver and install solution components
- Deliver user training

Close the Engagement

- Validate solution completion
- Create necessary documentation for operations
- Plan for ongoing operations of project
- Conduct post-project internal review
- Prepare final customer report and presentation
- Identify future opportunities
- Obtain references from customer

- Close the customer financial account
- Reward project team
- Obtain feedback from engagement team, customer staff, and partners
- Conduct internal postmortem
- Identify lessons leaned and action items for improving the project management methodology or service methodology
- Submit documents to solutions database for archival

among the components of the various services. By defining processes for the lowest-level activity, you can create a library of reusable building blocks to enhance productivity and service quality. Some components may be fairly general, such as requirements gathering. Other components may be more specific, such as identifying a company's system-tuning parameters. By creating methodology at a component level, consultants can pick and choose the component modules that best suit customer needs and adapt them accordingly.

The service components methodology may include:

- Process to perform service module activities
- Tools to speed service module delivery
- Templates and sample deliverables
- Best practices

Once the capabilities of PS are clearly defined, you can train the sales organization on how to mix and match these components to create solutions that meet customer needs.

Solutions methodology. The methodologies for project management, packaged services, and service components may be used by the consulting team to deliver engagements, and *not* promoted to customers. These methods and tools may be viewed as an important success factor and kept strictly proprietary.

At the same time, a "big picture" methodology is frequently *branded* and *promoted*, providing an important element of the group's value-add to customers. It may be called a solution methodology, professional services methodology, service delivery methodology, implementation methodology, or simply "our methodology" or "our approach." In some cases, the methodology applies to all services delivered by the organization

In addition, some consulting organizations have a methodology that is applied across a specific type of solution. For example, the IBM SOA Methodology is a method for developing service-oriented solutions. The high-level process flow consists of the following steps: (1) business modeling and transformation, (2) solution management (3) identification, (4) specification, (5) realization, (6) implementation, and (7) deployment, monitoring, and management. This type of methodology is also branded and promoted.

Create a Solutions Database

Knowledge acquired on a project can be applied to similar projects in the future if it is captured and organized. This knowledge, or intellectual property, allows consultants to learn from their peers, regardless of where they are located.

The practice of identifying and mapping intellectual assets within an organization is known as *knowledge management*. For the PS organization, the process requires someone on each major project— the project manager or a consultant—to gather the key information created for the engagement. Information should include a list of the project team members, the sales materials (e.g., customer presentation, proposal, statement of work), and the delivery materials (e.g., project plan, presentations, design documents, reports, training materials, and other customer deliverables). Best practices, tips and techniques, and lessons learned also should be captured. These materials are then stored in a centralized database or knowledgebase so they can be accessed by other sales teams or consultants working on similar projects.

Creating and maintaining this database requires headquarters personnel investment. These employees must solicit input from

PS engagement personnel to continually improve the information. Usually, the biggest challenge is getting consultants to submit the materials. The dilemma is that everyone wants to use the materials, but few people want to take the time to submit them. Once a project is completed, the engagement team immediately wants to move on to the next project. Management must encourage and reward information sharing. Make submission of materials a part of the team members' performance plans. Performance evaluations should recognize individuals who assist and support others both inside and outside their office.

Be Prepared to Invest

Product companies invest in developing and enhancing processes and procedures to ensure the quality of their products, but are often reluctant to invest in the training, methodology, databases, and tools that create efficiency and help ensure quality in consulting services. Most companies that invest in a new line of business expect it to be profitable—as fast as possible. A young professional services group is often faced with a chicken-and-egg problem: it must invest in people and services infrastructure to increase productivity and profits, while the company expects it to show a profit before it is willing to invest heavily in these areas.

In his book, *Managing the Professional Service Firm*, [13] David Maister describes three types of professional services practices:

1. *Expertise-based practice.* Success is highly dependent on hiring top-notch individuals with the skills and experience to devise unique solutions to solve complex business problems. Growth is often restricted by the availability of talent with the required credentials.

---

13. David H. Maister, *Managing the Professional Service Firm*, New York, NY: The Free Press, 1993.

2. *Experience-based practice.* These practices are built on the collective knowledge derived from past engagements. While hiring professionals with some skills and experience is still important, there is more reliance on training, methods, and best practices to build the requisite competencies and deliver proven solutions. Many technology companies use this model for their PS practices.

3. *Efficiency-based practice.* Less-experienced employees are trained to provide repeatable services. Practices rely on training, systems, and procedures to produce low-cost, fast, and predictable results. Margins are lower than other models and companies depend upon high volume to meet profit goals.

Your organization must decide which approach best meets your business goals. How much are you willing to invest in hiring top talent? In capitalizing on prior engagements? In developing methodology? In order to produce maximum efficiency, the decisions must be appropriately matched with the type of services your company provides to its customers. In addition, consider the size of your company, the maturity level, and the desired rate of growth.

Small software or hardware companies may be able to hire consultants with prior consulting experience and expertise in its core competencies. Instead of relying on an infrastructure of training, methodology, and quality processes to ensure success, a small organization may be successful relying on the professional involvements each of its consultants has had. These seasoned consultants can support sales efforts and help win deals over well-established companies with more junior personnel. To succeed, the company must attract, motivate, and reward these top consultants. The risks of relying on highly seasoned consultants include de-motivating them because they're not being challenged by unique situations, or overpaying individuals for jobs that could be done by more junior consultants.

New professional services organizations in larger companies often start out by hiring seasoned, skilled consultants who have a great deal of prior experience. As a company's success breeds more opportunities, it often reaches a point where it cannot grow as fast as it would like by hiring experienced talent. There must be investment in knowledge management, methodology, and training to develop less-experienced consultants and increase efficiency.

By being able to tap into the accumulated knowledge and experience of the entire services organization, companies can gain a real competitive advantage. Project management methodology, service delivery methodology, a solutions database, and a skills database are important resources to share.

In the late 1990s, IBM Global Services invested more than one billion US dollars a year in its services infrastructure. Many smaller organizations who are working hard to become profitable believe they cannot afford to invest much in training, methodology, and quality processes. Yet, the size and effectiveness of these organizations will always be limited if they don't find a way to build a services infrastructure to train and support consultants. If your company is serious about being successful in professional services, it must invest in creating the processes and databases to share information among its PS managers, engagement managers, and consultants worldwide.

Summary

Customers buy your expertise, proven methods for producing results, and your ability to apply technology to solve business problems. Just as companies invest in products to ensure good quality, you need to invest in your people, processes, and technology. This includes carefully selecting and training consultants, implementing a skills database, developing project management methodology, investing in service delivery methodology, and creating a solutions database.

Questions for Consideration

Does your company invest in its people, processes, and technology?

Companies invest in people and processes to provide quality products. Yet, they often fail to invest adequately in training, methodology, databases, and tools to create efficiency and ensure quality in professional services engagements. Here are some topics for consideration to evaluate your company's effectiveness in this area.

- How would you rate your consultants and project managers?
  - Do they have the required technical skills?
  - Do they have the necessary interpersonal skills?
  - Are poor performers developed and, if necessary, managed out?

- How effective is your PS recruiting?
  - Do you have a clear profile of each position that outlines the skills needed to be successful?
  - Are candidates well informed of the usual travel and work hours required in the job?
  - Are candidates selected for their interpersonal skills and attitude as well as their technical skills?

- How effective is your PS management at developing and retaining top talent?
  - Do consultants receive adequate training?
  - Are they assigned to projects where they can learn and grow?
  - Do they work with more senior people who can mentor them?
  - Are they effectively rewarded for a job well done?

- Does your PS group have a *skills database* to quickly locate both internal and third-party talent with the required skills to participate in an engagement? Is the database kept current?

- Does your PS organization invest in service delivery methodology?
    - For packaged services?
    - For service components or modules of services?

- Does your PS organization have a *solutions database* of reusable assets to capture and share sales and technical information, documents, and best practices from customer engagements? Is it kept current?

- Does your PS organization have processes and best practices to guide all aspects of a project from qualifying a prospect through the final steps necessary to close an engagement? Is it kept current?

- Does everyone in PS use the same methodology to sell, qualify, and manage projects?

12

Utilize Three Most Important Success Factors: Quality, Quality, Quality

You need a systematic program to ensure that customer expectations are met, as well as a way to measure success.

Quality must be the guiding principle for the PS business. Without high-quality service, marketing and sales efforts are ineffective. Marketing can enhance an organization's reputation, but it cannot fix an organization that is broken due to poor-quality work. Customer satisfaction is what PS organizations depend upon for repeat business and referrals. Customers base their satisfaction on the outcome as well as the service delivery process. You need a systematic program to consistently deliver customer satisfaction, as well as performance measurements to ensure accountability.

Importance of Quality Management

Quality management includes all the activities that organizations use to direct, control, and coordinate quality. These activities include:

- *Quality planning.* Setting quality objectives and developing processes to achieve those objectives

- *Quality assurance.* Activities to ensure that products or services satisfy customer requirements
- *Quality control.* Activities to ensure that quality requirements are actually being met
- *Quality improvement.* Activities that enhance an organization's ability to meet quality requirements

Products. In the product world, management would not consider developing a product until it established there was a market for it. And salespeople would not begin selling the product until the product was tested for quality. Companies institutionalize processes and procedures to ensure that products meet high quality standards. After the product is released, customer satisfaction surveys are conducted to measure the customer experience with the product. Based on the information gained, products are enhanced and new releases are made available. This systematic approach to bringing products to market is critical to producing high-quality products. And product companies became successful by building a reputation for providing high-quality products.

Services. Similar discipline is *required* in the services world—except the situation is reversed. With services, companies first *sell* a service and then *build* and *test* it. While product development engenders a disciplined approach, it is easier to sell a service and then discover that the expertise or processes are lacking to ensure quality delivery.

Product organizations have the opportunity to test their products before they leave the factory and correct defects without the customer's awareness. For services organizations, the customer site is the factory location. Providing quality results with services requires a greater sense of immediacy and discipline.

Service quality extends beyond service deliverables. Being able to meet the technical requirements outlined in a statement of work is one obvious measure of quality. However, consultants are also evaluated on non-technical criteria, such as responsiveness, meeting deadlines, keeping the customer informed, seeking approvals for changes in project scope, and other management and interpersonal factors. The relationship that a consulting team has with its customers is a key factor in customer perception of a quality service. The customer has to feel good about doing business with you.

Factors Affecting Service Quality

Some of the factors that make the quality of professional services challenging to manage and guarantee include the following:

- Intangible nature of services
- Dependence on customer involvement
- Quality is in the "eye of the beholder"
- Multiple stakeholders
- Size of delivery team
- Degree of innovation
- Skill depth and breadth

Intangible nature of services. As discussed earlier in this book, services cannot be seen or touched. The PS sales team sells a promise rather than an object. Because services are intangible and produced after the contract is signed and are usually developed at the customer site, it is substantially more challenging to control the quality of services than products.

Dependence on customer involvement. Most services require customer involvement in defining the problem, choosing the best approach to the problem, and developing the solution. This means that the consulting team is dependent upon the customer to provide good input and to make the time available to participate in interviews and review meetings, gather information, and whatever else is needed throughout the phases of the project.

Quality is in the "eye of the beholder." The ultimate measurement of quality is the customer perception of the service. This perception depends a great deal on the expectations of the customer. The less clear the customer is about what is needed and expected from PS, the harder it is to meet the expectations. Before the project begins, it is important to get clarity on the tasks and deliverables, discuss any assumptions (conditions you might take for granted), and delineate the roles and responsibilities of the customer team as well as the PS team. This information must be well documented in a statement of work in order to avoid misunderstandings. Be sure you understand which success criteria are most important to the customer and give particular consideration to those areas. In addition to service deliverables, consider the importance that the customer attaches to factors such as budget control, schedule control, and team communications.

Multiple stakeholders. The task of achieving customer satisfaction is compounded by the size of the project. In addition to satisfying the primary contact for the project, the PS team also must win the approval of other stakeholders in the company. This can be particularly challenging if the expectations of various stakeholders are not congruent. Holding a meeting with the all stakeholders at the beginning of the project can avoid any misconceptions.

Size of delivery team. Many professional services projects require a large team of people. The project team may include consultants from PS, subcontractors, customer employees, and possibly other consultants hired by the customer. The larger the project team, the more challenging it is to manage the quality of the project. A skilled project manager is a key factor for success. The best project managers are the best people managers. They know what needs to be done, the skills of the people involved, and how to marry them together. And they are skilled at motivating, team building, and mentoring.

Degree of innovation. When a service is well defined and similar to previous services delivered by PS, the PS team can set customer expectations about the service tasks, deliverables, timeframe, and quality with a fair degree of accuracy. However, when the work being performed is new to the PS team—and it must depend more heavily on its ability to devise new methods—it is more difficult to set clear expectations. Uncertainty also increases with the complexity of the project. Once again, a highly skilled engagement manager is needed to set expectations and manage any "curve balls" throughout the project. Building a solid relationship with the customer, based on trust, is crucial in getting through the rough spots along the way.

Skill depth and breadth. The more diverse the solution areas offered by a young organization, the more likely there will be engagements undertaken without the necessary skills to deliver quality results. In its eagerness to be successful, a new organization may take on projects that it doesn't have the skills to perform adequately. Eventually, the professional services organization learns the hard way: by being burned in a few failed engagements. Afterwards, the group becomes more selective about the projects it takes on and it begins building quality control procedures. However, at this point the PS organization's reputation may already be damaged in the eyes of the sales organization—and perhaps in the marketplace. Clearly, the appropriateness of projects must be agreed upon, and quality controls must be established before this type of unfortunate scenario plays itself out.

The factors above are common to *all* professional services—not simply high-tech professional services. Bente Lowendahl, a professor at the Norwegian School of Management, discusses many of these in more detail in her book *Strategic Management of Professional Service Firms.*[14]

---

14. Bente Lowendahl, B. R., *Strategic Management of Professional Service Firms.* Copenhagen, Denmark: Copenhagen Business School Press, 2000.

Results of Not Keeping the Service Promise

When PS signs a contract and provides an accompanying statement of work, it is making a commitment or promise to perform specific activities that result in defined deliverables to accomplish a customer's stated objectives. Over-promising undermines customer trust and can result in significant financial loss to the customer. For example, lack of an automated process can critically impede a conversion effort, or missing a project completion date can inflict a severe blow on a customer's holiday rush season.

Worst case, PS may find that it just cannot deliver results that meet the commitments established in the agreement. Anyone who has been involved in one of these "projects from hell" can attest to the penalties. Consultants involved in the project put in extensive time; top talent is often brought in to bail out the situation; and financial losses are incurred in attempting to salvage the project. Yet, by far, the most significant impact is customer dissatisfaction. Not only can a company end up losing a good customer, its PS organization can lose its credibility and reputation with other prospects.

Poor service quality also can affect the PS organization's reputation with the sales organization. It is as challenging, or sometimes even more difficult, to change the perception of your sales force than it is to change customer perception. Because technology companies often use the services of systems integrators or other service providers before building their own organization, the salesperson often has an alternative—she can call on the integrator or partner instead of her own PS organization.

If the competition hears about a failed project, they can use it against your company. And if the customer is large and the project is important, the news may even end up in major media outlets. In most cases, we learn lessons through our own experiences. Let's hope that your company can learn good practices from this book and avoid having to experience disastrous situations firsthand.

Just as dissatisfied customers can break a business, customers who are super satisfied can play a key role in making an organization successful. PS teams always need to perform at levels exceeding expectations—and yet stay within the planned budget constraints. Exceptional service can intensify customer loyalty to a point where customers virtually tune out competitive options. The real challenge is providing consistency in the quality of *all* engagements. Everyone in the consulting business understands that you're only as good as your last project.

Build Quality into the Process

In this section, we provide a brief description of some of the main methods that PS organizations can use to build quality into their sales and delivery processes.

Qualification: *Choose the right projects.* One of the key ways to assure that your customers will be satisfied is to decline projects that you don't have the skills to deliver adequately. Qualification procedures, including management reviews and approvals, must be built into your sales process and given serious attention. (See Chapter 9 for more information on this topic.)

Statement of work: *Set clear expectations.* The statement of work is the main vehicle for formally establishing clear expectations upfront. It describes the work objectives, approach, and deliverables or results. Any assumptions you make should be clearly stated as assumptions. Failure to discuss and document your assumptions explicitly can lead to problems later in the project.

The roles and responsibilities of your project team, as well as the customer project team, must be well-defined and made clear to the accountable parties. Misunderstandings can arise if you assume a key person in the customer organization will be working full-time on the project, while in reality customer management only plans to dedicate a few hours a week of the person's time.

TABLE 12.1 Statement of work subsections
(You can find another discussion of statement of work in Chapter 9.)

Component	Definition
■ Objectives	A summary of the project objectives
■ Project scope	The limit or boundary of the commitment
■ Project approach	The methodology or logical approach to be followed
■ Deliverables	The tangible results, of significant value, from the work performed
■ Project organization	The roles, responsibilities, and staff requirements of the service provider and the customer teams
■ Project schedule	The dates for the completion of each milestone and deliverable
■ Resources	The equipment and office space required for the project
■ Project controls	Project review control procedures
■ Risks/assumptions	Identified risks and assumptions that must be understood upfront and managed
■ Project price	The price and payment terms for the project
■ Assumptions	List of assumptions made during the planning process

The project schedule shows the dates for the completion of each deliverable and each milestone. It should also include a detailed schedule that shows the major tasks and dates for the tasks. The resources you require to do the project—such as office space, access to the building during late hours, or access to systems—must be documented.

The statement of work also sets expectations for how the engagement will be managed. It defines the project controls for change management, communication, project assessment, acceptance procedures, and issue management.

TABLE 12.2 Typical components for a PS project plan

- Execute summary
- Project strategy
    - Objectives
    - Project scope
    - Deliverables
    - Assumptions
- Project structure
    - Roles and responsibilities
- Project controls
    - Change management
    - Communications management
    - Quality management
    - Risk management
- Activities and estimates
- Resources (personnel, equipment, facilities)
- Project schedule (phases, milestones, timeline)
- Project oversight
    - Project reviews
    - Project document approvals
- Appendices and attachments

Project plan: *Manage customer expectations.* The statement of work defines customer expectations, and the project plan provides a tool to manage the project in order to meet those expectations. The project manager is responsible for producing and maintaining the project plan. It defines how the project will be performed (roles, responsibilities, activities), establishes the parameters for completion (timelines, phases, milestones), and defines the project controls to keep the project on track (change management, communications management, project reviews). All members of the project team should read and approve the project plan. As changes occur in the project, the project plan must be modified so it always remains current.

Project review meetings: *Keep the project on schedule.* After the SOW and the project plan are completed and accepted, regular review meetings keep the project team and customer management informed and the project on track. Commitments are confirmed and any obstacles in completing a task or deliverable on schedule are identified and discussed. Project review meetings also provide a forum for ongoing communications with customers to understand their expectations and concerns, to discuss any issues, and simply express appreciation to the project team. Be sure they are scheduled on a regular and frequent basis and that all key stakeholders commit to attend. Publish meeting minutes to give various parties another opportunity to keep informed. Minutes also serve to document activities. They keep everyone honest.

Topics discussed at weekly or biweekly meetings include:

- Project summary
- Status of each deliverable
- Discussion of issues and change requests
- Assignment of identified action items.

Project steering committee: *Keep key executives informed.* It is important to communicate with key customer executives throughout the project. For small projects, the customer sponsor who is accountable for the project may serve as the entire governing authority. For large projects, a steering committee, consisting of the sponsor plus key executives from relevant departments, is a good practice. Regular meetings with the steering committee keep executives informed of the project status and provide a means to efficiently resolve issues or gain approval for scope changes.

Project management: *Manage the project and project team.* Every project, no matter how large or small, needs an assigned single point of contact to orchestrate communications and resolve day-to-day project issues. Large projects need a dedicated project manager to ensure that the project is executed according to the project plan—

TABLE 12.3 Objectives for change management control

- Assess impact of changes on project schedules, resources, and price
- Provide a formal approval vehicle to proceed with change
- Establish impact of change
- Provide project audit log of all changes to the original scope

---

including quality, schedule, and budget requirements. The project manager also oversees the work of the project team. Proper communications methods between the project manager and the customer are critical for project success. This includes regular communications, project review meetings, issue-management controls, and project status reports. Formal project management methodology is also extremely important for large projects.

Change management: *Manage scope creep.* Although tasks and deliverables are defined upfront in the statement of work, the customer may request additional work. Or some aspects of the project may indicate that further work is required. Or revised priorities, new technology, or staff reorganization may affect the project scope. In any case, it is important to ensure that the proper change control procedures are understood and implemented. The change control method should be reviewed with the customer during the sales cycle. During project delivery, if the assumptions or project scope change to a significant degree, most likely the project price also needs to change. In a fixed-price project, this becomes important in order to ensure profitability. And even if the project is being billed on a time and materials basis, changes in the project scope that affect the billing or the schedule must be reviewed and approved.

Any requested changes from the project scope described in the SOW should be processed using the agreed-upon change management process. Even if you decide to include a change with no additional fee, documenting the change and its monetary value prompts the customer to recognize and appreciate the additional work that is being provided.

Acceptance procedures: *Get sign-off.* Customers expect that the deliverables defined in the statement of work will be completed on schedule and will meet their quality expectations. In order to manage customer expectations, it is important to get sign-off on each deliverable. At the end of the project, a final acceptance letter formally notifies the customer that all deliverables have been provided, specifies the official contract closure date, and thanks the customer for his dedication and commitment to the project. It is important to get final sign-off so there is a clear understanding that the project is officially completed and all contractual obligations have been met.

Issue management: *Keep molehills from growing into mountains.* A breakdown in communication is at the root of many project failures. A situation that starts out as a small technical problem or personnel issue can easily grow into a major political nightmare if it is not managed properly. Be sure that your consultants know that they can always come to management with problems. Customer calls from angry customers should never be a surprise.

Formal escalation process: *Ensure quick problem resolution.* A formal issue escalation process for reporting problems to PS management is required to ensure that the appropriate people are informed and issues are resolved in a timely manner. These issues may pertain to the schedule, resources, deliverables, technical or performance problems, or any other issues that may impact the project or customer satisfaction.

Risk assessment: *Manage the areas of exposure.* A risk assessment should be conducted during the qualification phase of a sale, during the development of a proposal, during project start-up, and periodically throughout the delivery of a project. Risk management is accomplished by anticipating possible areas where the engagement may be vulnerable and proactively planning ways to manage the risk. Risk elements may be financial, legal, or political. They may be related to the project definition, project size or schedule, project personnel (internal, subcontractor or customer), customer commitment, quality management, technical requirements, or project environment. A checklist is useful to identify the risks associated with a project. The key to controlling risks is to identify them early, reassess them throughout the engagement using a systematic procedure, and develop plans to manage and mitigate the risks.

For each risk that is identified, a plan is needed to manage the risk. For example, if there is risk involved because the schedule is aggressive, the risk management plan may be defined as follows:

- Prioritize requirements
- Maintain firm control over scope
- Develop a contingency plan
- Define milestones and deliverables
- Conduct more frequent management reviews
- Assign an experienced project team.

Heightened risk awareness—and contingency plans—could lead to some project reorganizing and personnel shifts, and should be expected.

Project audit: *Get a second opinion.* Despite the best efforts of the project team and the use of project control measures, such as project review meetings and issue management escalation, projects can still get off track. When this happens, it is time to get a second opinion. PS management may decide to bring in an audit team to diagnose why a project is not meeting its financial or performance goals. At other times, an audit may be used as a preventative measure to ensure that the project is on track. Or it may be used strictly as a quality control measure to ensure that the project team is on target. A standard project audit checklist is useful to ensure that all elements of the project are covered. The larger and more significant the project and the customer, the more important it is that an audit be performed.

TABLE 12.4 Standard methods to manage project quality

Process	Objective	Stage
Qualification process	Choose right projects	Sales
Statement of work	Set clear expectations	Contract
Project plan	Manage expectations	Delivery
Project review meetings	Keep project on schedule	Delivery
Project steering committee	Keep executives informed	Delivery
Project management	Manage project/ project team	Delivery
Change management	Manage scope creep	Delivery
Acceptances procedures	Get sign-off	Delivery
Issue management	Resolve problems quickly	All
Escalation process	Get management involved	All
Risk assessment	Manage areas of exposure	All
Project audit	Get a second opinion	Delivery

Learn from Your Experiences

Customer engagements can last many months or even years. When the project is finished, the team members are anxious to move on to something new. Nevertheless, it is crucial to capture the wisdom and lessons learned from the project.

Project review. Conduct an internal project review with the team and management to evaluate and measure the overall project, team performance, and the effectiveness of the processes and procedures. This is a good time to recommend process improvements.

Knowledge capture. In a business where knowledge and experience are assets, it is important to capture the documents and lessons learned. The project description, project documents, and the lessons learned must be submitted for inclusion in the company's solutions database (knowledgebase). To ensure that this happens, include this task in project managers' or consultants' job descriptions and discuss it during employees' annual performance reviews.

Analyze lost business opportunities. In situations where you compete for consulting projects and lose, it is important to understand why you lost. Take the time to meet with the prospect to understand how he perceives your strengths and weaknesses, and why you lost the business. Or consider hiring a third-party to conduct the analysis in order to ensure you are getting objective information.

Quality manager. Strong leadership is important to create a culture that is dedicated to quality and continuous improvement of engagement performance. Clearly, practice managers and engagement managers play a key role in fostering and managing quality in the organization. In addition, consider adding a PS quality manager to monitor and enhance quality. Because services are delivered by people, you can expect errors and problems to occur along the way. If they are handled properly, they can lead to an even closer relationship with the customer. If an organization is large enough to warrant one, a quality manager can assist the local practice managers and engagement managers in effectively managing and resolving problems at accounts.

Solicit Customer Feedback

Perception is reality. Customer perception of the work performed during an engagement is the prime measure of quality. And a customer's perception of the results is directly related to his expectations, as well as his relationship with the project team. So even if PS believes the solution delivered was technically superior, the customer may not be satisfied if the project was delayed, exceeded the planned budget, or did not meet his expectations for a variety of reasons.

Earlier in this chapter, we presented methods to control and enhance the quality of a project throughout the engagement. In addition, it is important to measure the quality from the customer perspective when the project is completed. If customers are not satisfied, they will find other organizations to meet their future needs. Thus, low customer satisfaction is a leading indicator of future decline, even though the current financial picture may look positive.

Customer debriefing. A final project review with the customer team and management is important to obtain concurrence on the completion of the tasks and deliverables, close out any remaining issues, and get feedback on the overall project—what went well, what could be improved.

It is also important for the practice manager, or other senior manager who was not involved in the day-to-day project activities, to meet with the main customer contact to obtain his feedback on the team members and the overall project. The customer may be willing to share some input with senior management that he is not willing to share with the team directly. These meetings provide input to deal with issues relating to individual resources or miscommunications or missed expectations at the project level. They also provide important input for ideas to improve future projects. If a meeting is positive, this is a good time to ask to use the account as a reference. If the customer is willing, this is also a good time to schedule a video interview with the customer executives. These meetings also provide an opportunity to learn about new customer problems or challenges where your team may contribute.

Customer satisfaction surveys. The importance of customer satisfaction cannot be overemphasized. PS should contract with an independent organization to gather input quarterly from a representative sample of customers. Too often companies ask their sales force to pick some of their customers to complete a survey. Because they naturally pick their best and most satisfied customers, the results are skewed.

Customers may be more willing to share some information when they know that it will remain anonymous. These surveys allow management to compare the quality of work in various geographies

TABLE 12.5 Sample factors to include in
customer-satisfaction surveys

Overall rating
- Overall satisfaction
- Likelihood to buy again
- Likelihood to recommend

About the service outcome
- Quality of service deliverables
- Objectives reached

About delivery
- Timeliness of delivery
- Effectiveness of service tools
- Transfer of knowledge

About project team
- Competence
- Responsiveness
- Reliability
- Relations
- Communication
- Confidentiality
- Courtesy

About price
- Price relative to quality

worldwide, within types of practices, and progress over time. Hopefully, the results will be so positive that they can be used by marketing to promote the exceptionally high-quality work of your organization. Happy customers provide referrals and can contribute significantly to market penetration.

Customer base analysis.   Periodically, conduct an analysis to determine which of your customers provide the most revenue and profits. Take a close look at these customers. What industries do they represent? What types of services do they purchase? Why do they continue to buy services from your company? Understand why you are successful, so you can repeat the success factors in other areas of your services business.

Summary

Quality is the guiding principle of the PS business. To ensure quality of *all* engagements, you need to build quality into the sales and delivery processes through qualification procedures for selecting engagements, statements of work, project reviews, change management, final acceptance procedures, issue management processes, and project audits. It is also important to measure quality through customer debriefings and satisfaction surveys.

Questions for Consideration

Does your professional services organization invest in quality?

Companies create processes and procedures to manage the quality of their products. Yet, many often fail to invest adequately in the quality of their professional services. Here are some questions for consideration to evaluate the quality of your professional services business.

- How would you rate the quality of the services provided by your PS organization?
    - ○ Is the quality consistent across practices?
    - ○ Is the quality consistent worldwide?
    - ○ How does your sales organization perceive the quality of your professional services engagements?
    - ○ What is your organization's reputation for quality in the marketplace?

- What methods does your organization use to build quality into your sales and delivery efforts?
    - ○ Use qualification procedures during the sales process?
    - ○ Set clear expectations in the statement of work?
    - ○ Manage customer expectations with a comprehensive project plan?
    - ○ Use project reviews to keep the project on track?
    - ○ Employ change management procedures?
    - ○ Get sign-off on acceptance of deliverables?
    - ○ Institute formal escalation procedures to manage issues?
    - ○ Implement risk assessments?
    - ○ Conduct project audits?

- How are the results from a project used to contribute to the quality of similar future projects?
    - Is an internal project review meeting held with the project team to measure team performance and discuss lessons learned?
    - Are the documents and lessons learned captured and stored in a database?

- After a project is completed, is customer feedback captured?
    - Is a final project review meeting held with the customer to obtain concurrence on completion of the tasks and deliverables, get final sign-off, and obtain feedback on the overall project?
    - Does a senior manager in PS meet with customers to obtain feedback and learn about potential new projects?
    - Does the company contract a third-party research firm to gather quarterly or semi-annual input from representative customers?

13

Manage
Partner Relationships

*Paramount to success, PS must align its partner strategy with the
corporate partner strategy for one unified partner strategy.*

To paraphrase a famous saying, a technology vendor cannot be all
things to all customers. In today's complex business environment,
many companies increasingly depend on outside alliances. Companies
form partnerships to harness the competencies of other companies
without incurring the costs of bringing these competencies in-house.
Despite issues and challenges, partner relationships can be very
successful when you put into place well-defined plans and processes.
Your PS organization must define the role, if any, that channel and
alliance partners will play in selling and delivering your services. To
define your partner program, ask yourself these questions:

- What are the objectives for your partner program?
- What are the strategies and tactics?
- Who will manage the program?
- How will you select your partners?
- Will you certify partners?
- What is the relationship between your PS partner program
  and your corporate channels and alliances organization?

Partnering relationships is a complex topic that deserves a full book to do it justice. This chapter will highlight some of the key factors to consider when developing a professional services partner program and teaming with partners.

Nature of Partnering

Partnering involves an agreement between two or more organizations to cooperate in a specific business activity. Resellers, value-added resellers, systems integrators, independent software vendors, and original equipment manufacturers, are common types of partner structures. See Table 13.1 for a definition of these terms.

For a partnership to be successful and sustainable, both parties must be clear on the goals of the relationship. There must be value for each partner as well as a compelling value proposition for the joint customer. Partners must also be prepared to invest in partner management, co-marketing, co-selling, training, certification, or other partner development programs.

Partner program benefits include broader market reach, cost savings from shared marketing, incremental revenue, superior business solutions, competitive advantage, and prestige gained from being associated with a partner. Professional services organizations can also gain application or industry expertise, and the flexibility to better manage the supply and demand of consultants.

When teaming to deliver professional services engagements, your organization can act either as a prime contractor or a subcontractor. As a prime contractor, you provide overall engagement management, architecture, and perhaps some technical skills, while subcontracting the remaining activities to partners. As a subcontractor, you provide activities and deliverables that leverage your specific skills (and that are complementary and non-threatening to your partner's skills) within the context of a larger engagement lead by a partner.

TABLE 13.1 Types of partners

Partner Type	Definition
Reseller	Company that resells your products or services
Value-added-reseller (VAR)	Company that adds some value (product features or professional services) to your existing product and then resells it as an integrated product or solution
Systems integrator (SI)	Company that specializes in building systems for clients by combining hardware and software products from multiple vendors
Independent software vendor (ISV)	Company that makes and sells software products that run on your hardware or software platforms
Original equipment manufacturer (OEM)	Company that embeds technology or a component made by a second company in its own product, or sells the product of the second company under its own brand

Partner Program Objectives

Depending on what is to be achieved and the focus of your company, there are different reasons to partner with other companies.

Product-centric companies utilize resellers to assist in the sales of products for many reasons, including:

- Meet financial objectives
- Increase product sales
- Promote new products
- Increase product sales in specific geographies
- Reach new target markets and customers
- Decrease costs

Professional services organizations create partnerships to assist in the sales and delivery of services for similar reasons. They include the following:

- Boost company capacity for selling and delivering services
- Increase resources in specific geographical locations or competencies
- Broaden competencies by bringing in delivery resources with new skills
- Increase sales and delivery resources for branded packaged services
- Reach new target markets and customers
- Jointly develop, sell, and deliver new solutions
- Decrease costs

Be sure you are clear about what you want to gain from your partner relationships before taking steps to hire partners.

Partner Program Ownership

Like any relationship, professional services partnerships require careful management to keep the relationships moving forward, to alleviate unnecessary conflict and complications, and to make sure the customer is well taken care of. This requires program ownership with clear strategies, objectives, and communications.

Corporate vs PS program. Product companies typically invest heavily in partnerships with VARs, systems integrators, and other partners. Usually there is a centralized business development or channels organization in headquarters to manage these relationships. Although this department is responsible for the company's channel and alliance programs relating to products, it is extremely important that the PS organization get involved in setting the partner strategies and operations relating to selling and delivering professional services.

Management needs to determine the level of investment and

ownership for the PS partner program. Will the *corporate* channels group set up your partner relationships with systems integrators and subcontractor agreements with VARs? Or will *PS* handle its own partner relationships? In either case, you need to empower at least one individual within the managing organization with the responsibility for championing and driving the PS partner strategies and programs.

One unified partner strategy. If you decide to have a separate PS partner organization, the group must integrate its partner strategies with the corporate and product partner strategies. *It is crucial to have one overall partner strategy* so that there is clear alignment throughout all partner relationships and agreements and a unified partner policy for the corporation.

PS corporate vs local practices. In the desire to set up a profitable business, professional services practices look for ways to put more "feet on the street" while minimizing overhead. Too often, partnering is handled locally with each practice setting up its own relationships with systems integrators and subcontractors. The lack of clear strategy and implementation plans at an enterprise level results in failed partnerships and lost profits, and can even impact customer relationships.

Determine what roles and responsibilities will be handled at the corporate level versus at the area or district level. Typically, master partner agreements (containing terms and conditions that govern the relationship companywide) are developed at a corporate level, whereas the day-to-day operations of working with sales and delivery partners are better managed by area or district staff.

In order to ensure the success of your PS partner program, select an individual to be responsible for the strategy and ongoing management of the overall program. If your organization is small, this same individual may also be the contact for each of the partner relationships. Large companies usually have a business development manager assigned to one or several partners.

Building Services Partner Programs

There is often a high rate of partnership failure when partnerships are built haphazardly. But with careful construction by the organizing company and the partner, both parties can achieve their objectives.

Partner strategy. A well-defined strategy is paramount to the success of a professional services partner program. Too many companies just jump right in and start hiring partners without first defining the program's goals, objectives, procedures, practices, and measurements. Often these topics are only given consideration after conflicts or failures make the need for planning painfully apparent.

You must set expectations and define roles and responsibilities upfront. The guidelines should encompass a wide range of circumstances throughout the life cycle of an engagement, including:

- Relationship management
- Sales calls
- Prime contractor and subcontractor teaming agreement
- Contractual processes
- Packaged services
- Knowledge transfer
- Competitive situations

Partner selection. Partners vary in size, structure, importance to the company, and in various other ways. To ensure that you and potential partner organizations will make a good match, establish comprehensive evaluation criteria. Some of the factors to consider include:

- Technical competencies
- Compatibility of goals
- Cultural fit
- Track record for achieving customer satisfaction
- Company characteristics (e.g., financial stability, geographical coverage)

By definition, a partnership is a "win-win" proposition. Both partners must invest in making the partnership a success. Clearly, a partnership in which one partner's investments or gains far exceed the other will not last very long. Be sure you and your partner have identified what you want from the relationship.

Multi-tiered programs. To accommodate partners who vary in size, roles, and level of strategic importance, most companies establish a multi-tiered channel partner program. The models used for tiered programs vary from company to company. Benefits are structured to recognize partners' investment in and contribution to selling and delivering solutions that drive joint success. The higher the partnership level, the greater the combined commitment required to sustain program momentum.

Partner investment. Frequently, companies forget that partnerships are about quality, not quantity. Signing up a large number of partners without the strategy and resources to manage the relationships adequately is a sure path to failure. Focus on a few key relationships and make them successful before expanding the program.

Partnerships do not represent a free lunch for the PS organization. A signed partnership agreement marks just the beginning of the investment. Be sure to allocate adequate funding and resources for training, co-marketing, co-selling, and other joint efforts. Management at all levels must support the program financially and in practice. Invest the resources, funding, and time to make your partner program successful.

Partner measurement. Just as you need to survey your customers to measure their satisfaction with your services and their commitment to your company, you also need to measure partner satisfaction and loyalty. Conduct surveys that gauge overall satisfaction, value of the partnership, communications, channel conflict, problem resolution, marketing support, training, and ease of doing business. Additionally, be sure to include questions in customer discussions and surveys to measure customer satisfaction with partner products and services. By obtaining feedback from partners and customers, you can improve partnering management and relationships, identify which partners should be retained, and determine how you can assist them to achieve the highest level of success.

Partner Program Pitfalls

The success of any partner program depends a great deal on how it is structured and how well your organization deals with partner problems before they get out of control. Let's take a look at some of the most common situations that could present problems for you and your partners.

Who's on first—you or your partner? Many product companies (without a PS organization) initially provide consulting services to their customers through systems integrators or other outside service providers. Salespeople introduce the service providers to their customers, and customers choose whom they would like to hire. At this point, there is no competition between the vendor and its partners; the vendor provides products and the service provider delivers services.

When you create your own PS organization, you must determine how to align yourself with your partners to prevent channel conflict. In today's business environment, companies are competing one day and cooperating the next. If a systems integrator is promoting a product from one of your competitors as part of a solution that you have nothing do with, it is logical for you to compete against the firm—with both products and services—if the opportunity is in your marketplace. However, if the systems integrator is promoting your company's products, it makes more sense to allow your partner to win the deal and to team with them, if possible, in the service delivery. In other words, your partner takes the lead. Be sure you have a clear policy for handling sales situations that involve partners when they're in competition with you and that your sales organization understands your company's position.

Intellectual property. When your hire partners to assist in delivering your services, you may need to provide them with intellectual property—proprietary methodology and tools—to enable them to do quality work. To protect your intellectual property, consider the following:

- Who will define and manage your IP management processes?
- What are your policies for licensing your IP?
- Is IP properly protected in your partner agreements?
- How frequently do partners need to renew their IP licenses?
- Will IP be provided for free or a fee?

This is a complex topic. Seek legal assistance to analyze and address all the issues related to intellectual property.

Partner communications. Good communications between your company and your partners is essential for success. Too often, the only time a technology provider and a partner communicate is to resolve problems or haggle over co-marketing dollars. Communicate through your channel partner managers, your website, sales materials, newsletters, and training programs. Through clear and ongoing communications you can enhance the effectiveness of your partners' sales and delivery efforts, and build partner loyalty. Respect, understanding, trust, and teamwork are all important for a successful collaboration.

Types of Partner Relationships

The main ways in which partners collaborate with professional services organizations include the following:

- Sell packaged services
- Sell custom services
- Deliver packaged services
- Serve as subcontractors
- Serve as prime integrator
- Co-develop services
- Provide third-party products for resale

Sell packaged services. Packaged services with your brand are the easiest services for third-party service providers to resell. Service briefs and other collateral are often available to help explain the service. There is a predefined list of the service activities and deliverables, as well as the number of consultants and time required to deliver the service. Packaged services usually have a fixed price so it is easy for customers to get a complete picture of exactly the level of investment that is required and what they will get for their money.

Sell custom services. When your partner is selling a custom service, it is recommended that a business development manager or engagement manager from the PS organization get involved early to ensure that the service and customer needs match, the service deliverables and activities are understood, the customer role is clear, and the appropriate resources are available for delivery on the de-sired dates. Unless a service provider's sales team is highly skilled at selling professional services, they will most likely find it difficult to sell your custom services.

Deliver packaged services. If a packaged service has well-defined methods and supporting tools, you can more easily train and certify third-party consultants to deliver them. (See "certification" later in this chapter.) Whether you use your own staff or partners to deliver your packaged services, supply and demand must be aligned. I have seen situations where agreements are signed, consultants are certified, and then there is not sufficient demand for the packaged service to fully utilize the trained consultants. After a service is delivered, it is also crucial to measure the performance of the consultants to ensure customer satisfaction.

Serve as subcontractors (you are prime). If your PS organization provides project management for engagements and serves as the prime contractor, you may decide to hire subcontractors to supplement your organization's available resources, or to provide expertise in a specific competency, industry, or business solution. In order to get subcontractor input on the solutions and include their profiles in your proposal, you may need to identify these consultants before the business is won. Master teaming agreements with ISVs, VARs, or other service providers will expedite this process.

Your PS organization must carefully manage the subcontractor relationships. For each engagement, the subcontractors need to provide a statement of work (SOW) that defines their activities, deliverables, assumptions, fees, and length of the project. Procedures are necessary to manage legal contracts, time cards, and invoicing, and to comply with government laws and regulations. Procedures are also required to manage and measure the subcontractor's work.

Serve as prime (you are subcontractors). No one knows a company's products and technologies, and how they can be implemented, better than the vendor's employees. This makes a vendor's consultants valuable resources to support systems integrators who are delivering services related to your company's products and solutions. For example, if a systems integrator is providing a solution that will run on Sun Microsystems hardware, Sun Microsystems consultants are likely candidates to serve as subcontractors to integrate the platform. If your consultants are working as subcontractors, you must create the proper legal agreements, including statements of work, to establish the terms and conditions of the teaming relationship. You must also offer consultant rates that meet the prime integrator's margin requirements for subcontractors and still allow your organization to make a profit.

Co-develop services. In order to gain synergy from the combined talents of two companies, an alliance may be formed to develop joint solutions that are sold by both companies. It is extremely important that the roles and responsibilities of each company are well defined and documented upfront in order to set expectations.

Provide third-party products for resale. As you integrate solutions for customers, you may likely recommend specific products that are not offered by your company. To provide your customers with one-stop-shopping service, you can become a reseller of these third-party products. The customer wins by easily and quickly purchasing the product without any effort on his part. You win by purchasing the product at a discount, selling it at retail rate, and making a profit. To do this effectively, you need to select vendors, sign reseller agreements, establish communication mechanisms, and track revenue per vendor.

Certification for Sales and Delivery Partners

IT certification programs are commonly provided by large hardware and software vendors to train and qualify partners to sell and deliver their services. Large corporations such as IBM, Microsoft, Hewlett-Packard, Sun, and Cisco have certification programs. Many medium-sized companies are also adopting this practice.

Consultants can hold certifications related to specific job roles, such as systems administration or database administration, or for roles in delivering specific services. Role-based training programs are usually offered at various skill levels such as associate, intermediate, or advanced. PS organizations may develop and deliver their own training, authorize an outside training company to provide it, or endorse an existing certification program for a standard technology.

Typically, companies hire test service providers to administer the written tests. If available, Web-based practice tests allow candidates to assess their skill levels and readiness prior to taking the actual test.

Some PS organizations charge partners to attend their training programs; others provide the training for free. Although revenue can be received from training and certification, there still must be an initial investment to launch a certification program.

Summary

Well-defined strategies are needed to map out the roles, responsibilities, and behaviors for partner relationships. Whether you team with partners to sell your services, deliver your services, co-deliver your services, or co-develop your services, be sure you have a clear strategy. Integrate it with the corporate partner strategy, implement and fund the program, and designate someone to manage the program in order to pave the road to success.

Questions for Consideration

Does your professional services organization effectively manage partner relationships?

Professional services organizations typically team with systems integrators, ISVs, VARs, or other service providers. It is crucial that these relationships be well managed in order to ensure customer satisfaction. Here are some topics for consideration to evaluate your partner relationships.

- In what ways do partners support your professional services organization?
  - Sell services
  - Sell custom services
  - Deliver packaged services
  - Deliver custom services
  - Serve as subcontractors
  - Serve as the prime integrator
  - Co-develop and deliver joint services

- Do you have a clear strategy and implementation program for partnering, including the following:
  - Program goals and objectives
  - Partner selection criteria
  - Operational procedures and practices
  - Process to manage intellectual property
  - Measurements

- Is the PS partner program well aligned with your corporate channels and alliances program?

- Is the program well managed?
  - Is there a professional responsible for the overall PS partner program?
  - Are managers assigned to coordinate the relationship with individual partners?
  - Is the program adequately funded?
  - Is a marketing professional assigned to plan and implement joint marketing programs with partners?

- How would you rate the quality of your alliances and teaming agreements?

- Does your PS organization have a certification program?
  - Do you certify individuals for specific job roles or services?
  - Does your company deliver its own training, authorize an outside training company, or endorse a standard certification program?
  - Do you charge partners to attend certification training classes?
  - How frequently do you require partners to be re-certified?
  - Do you charge partners to use your intellectual property?

14

Manage Business Operations

Professional services leaders must master a difficult balance—meeting the needs of customers, employees, and partners, while ensuring revenue and cost targets.

E ven with a smart business strategy, committed employees and partners, and interested customers, it's not enough to run a moneymaking PS business. To win the chance to compete and deliver engagements successfully year after year, PS leaders must balance customer, employee, and partner responsibilities, while *effectively running business operations to achieve its revenue and profit goals.*

This chapter identifies the experience a good leader brings to the business and focuses on two crucial topics to maximize profitability: setting services prices and balancing resource supply with demand.

Hire Experienced Leaders

As we have discussed throughout this book, there is a huge difference between a product business and a human-capital-intensive services business. Most product companies fail to realize the differences and tend to underestimate the challenges and the investment needed to build a successful services business. When starting a new professional services business in a product-centric company, in-house product talent alone is often not prepared to build and run the business. Companies usually need to hire managers with professional services experience—and, ideally, managers with experience managing a professional services business in a product company. In PS organizations, these leaders have had to manage a project-based business, balance supply and demand, leverage the organization's collective knowledge, craft solutions to unique customer problems, and establish service metrics and accounting practices. They're experienced in the ways of PS, which are very different from the modes of activity in a product-only environment.

Leaders who are recruited from consulting firms have a huge learning curve. They need to build strong relationships with their counterparts in the product business and adjust to the culture of a product-centric company. Unfortunately, services managers are not usually welcomed with open arms. Their product peers achieved success by creating, marketing, and selling products, and they frequently view services as a necessary evil. PS managers need to educate them on the services business and find ways to demonstrate how services help sell products, ensure customer satisfaction with the products, result in more devoted customers, and contribute to corporate profits. A good way for a new manager to start is by meeting with executives, product managers, sales managers and customers; understanding their challenges; and learning what they expect of the PS organization. Developing strong relationships with product peers is a key success factor.

Let Price Reflect Your Value

Pricing is one of the many factors in a services business that differs from a product business. The more complex the service, the less likely price is one of the most important factors to your customers. Few people are looking for the lowest-priced brain surgeon. Likewise, companies are willing to pay top dollar for services that are critical to their success or must be completed in a short time. An online toy company that needs its Web operations functional for the holiday buying season is motivated to pay a higher price in return for peace of mind that the project will be completed on schedule.

Price is one indicator of quality. Companies that provide superior service have a greater opportunity to demand a premium price. In fact, the higher the price, the higher the customer perceives the quality. This is true for products, but even more so for services. With products, the customer has the opportunity to evaluate the quality of something concrete before purchasing. Whereas with services, the lack of tangible attributes makes price an even more important indicator of quality.

Avoid the low-price position in professional services. If the customer is shopping for the lowest price, even if you win one engagement, there is always someone else who could come along and offer a lower price next time around. There is no customer loyalty in these situations. And these customers often turn out to be the most demanding and least grateful.

The more complex and innovative the service, the less likely price is a factor for the customer. Whereas, for simple services that have a high degree of standard processes, low price and performance efficiency are usually the more important decision factors when customers are selecting a service provider.

Price can raise customer expectations or lower them. By setting prices too low, you can potentially devalue your services in the eyes of your customers. Prices set too high can be perceived as providing poor value for the money. When you are setting prices, you are also sending a message to the customer about service quality.

Attach value to "free" services. A product company may discount an assessment service to learn more about the customer's environment and requirements, or give away an installation service to sell hardware or software. If the service is provided for free or significantly discounted, it is a good idea to present the actual price of the service and even send a bill that shows the service price with the entire amount credited. This helps establish the value of the service and reinforces the fact that your company provided a billable service at no charge. If the sales organization is the group that will benefit from the hardware or software sale, the professional services group should consider negotiating an agreement to cross-charge the sales organization for services provided at no-charge to the customer. This will help ensure that no-charge services are only being offered when there is profitable return in the current product sale or expectation of a future profit to justify the free service.

Another option is to charge the customer for the assessment, but agree to provide a credit for the full price of the assessment service if the customer purchases a follow-on implementation service. This helps eliminate free-loading customers who are not serious about doing additional services business with your company.

Discounting policies. Some companies take a firm position that their consulting fees are non-negotiable. This policy eliminates possible disputes and presents a more professional image. Other companies set their fees high and regularly discount them. Another alternative is to discount the hardware or software associated with the service. Because products are more easily measured against competitor products than services are, discounting the product instead of the service can help position your products as more price competitive. To discourage your sales force from discounting professional services, reduce the commission on the entire deal if it includes discounted services.

It is also important to know how discounting affects the bottom line. Be sure to track the discount percentages on engagements so you can determine if profits are being impacted by sales discounts versus scope creep or other factors related to project delivery.

When a product salesperson is not successful in selling consulting services, his favorite excuse is that the service price is too high. Over the years, I have seen many surveys regarding what customers value most when selecting services. Expertise is always at the top, and price is always low on the scale. Your price is not too high just because some of your salespeople say it's too high. They need to start *focusing on selling the value*—not the price. When you demonstrate an understanding of the customer's problem and the customer perceives the value of your proposed solution and your team's ability to deliver it, closing the sales is easy.

Bundling hours. To make it easier for companies to purchase your services, consider offering bundles of hours to be used during a specific time period established by the customer. Bundling service hours helps managers:

- Plan ahead and gain approval during the optimal time in their budget process or ordering cycle
- Gain approval for services at the time a product order is approved
- Later launch small service projects quickly without a lengthy approval process

Offering a discounted hourly rate for the bundle of hours makes the package even more attractive to managers. Assigning a *product number* to a fixed unit of hours provides a way to bill for professional services that can easily fit within the constraints of a product company's billing system.

Set Pricing—T&M or Custom Quote

Professional services organizations have two main approaches to setting fees for services: (1) charge for the time spent working on a project, or (2) provide an upfront quote for a project. There are pros and cons for each approach—from your perspective and the customer's perspective (see Table 14.1). Young professional services organizations usually begin with hourly billing, move to cost-based pricing, and then to value pricing as they become more established and experienced.

Time-and-materials pricing. Without a track record, it is difficult to scope a project and provide a fixed price. For this reason, new professional services organizations should start by charging for projects by *time and materials* (T&M) expended. With time-and-materials pricing, a services organization bills for services based on the time expended on the project, plus the expenses incurred in delivering the project (e.g., travel, equipment). Most consulting companies have a range of consulting fees based on the seniority and expertise of the consultant.

Your project proposal should include an estimate of the total hours and costs. If the project is taking longer than anticipated, tell the customer why your estimate is changing and by how much. Perhaps unexpected problems were incurred or the customer requested additional work. Good change control management is critical regardless of the pricing method.

Cost-based pricing. Cost-based pricing is one method of determining a fixed price for a project. Calculate the total service cost and add an additional amount to achieve the expected profit margin. Be sure to consider all service costs, including the number of consultants assigned to the engagement, their level of expertise, the time required by each consultant to do the job, travel expenses, and cost of the methodology. Usually, a risk factor is included in the equation. You may want to include a bonus fee for completing the project ahead of schedule.

Experienced consulting groups can estimate small projects based on past engagements. If the project is large, professional services organizations usually charge for an assessment service to gain the required information to scope the project. The assessment service provides recommendations for the customer. And the information gained during the assessment should be sufficient to prepare a proposal for an implementation service with a fixed-price quote or at least a price for the next phase of the project. The customer is billed in accordance with the contract terms (e.g., at completion of a deliverable, milestone, phase, entire project).

Value-based pricing. In value-based pricing, a price is set based on the value of the service to the customer. The fee is earned when the agreed-upon goal is achieved; it is not dependent upon the amount of time expended. To determine a value-based price, start by calculating the project cost and applying the minimum profit margin to obtain the lowest possible price you can accept. Then consider the value added and the price you believe the customer will accept. The challenge is arriving at a price for a project that appears fair to the prospect and is sufficiently profitable for your organization.

To successfully use value-based pricing, you must comprehend the value your service creates for the customer and convince your customer of that value. This requires experience, business savvy, and top-notch sales skills. Some of the factors that contribute to perception of value follow:

- *Know what your customer values most.* Your customer may be most interested in reducing costs, or increasing competitiveness, or creating a new source of revenue. Or the customer's main focus may be a solution that is delivered quickly to accommodate the increase in customer volume during the holiday season. The better you understand exactly what your customer hopes to achieve from the engagement, the more closely you can align your proposal to these goals.

- *Demonstrate your competence.* To justify the price of your service, show that you understand the customer's issues and how to solve them. If significant challenges are involved, point out the risks, how you will manage them, and walk the customer through your plans to complete the project on schedule. If you have a unique methodology, emphasize how your investment in methods and tools will reduce project time, costs, and risks.

- *Share valuable insights.* Identify issues or ways to improve financial performance that were unknown to the customer.

This requires knowledge of the customer business, as well as effective questioning and careful listening to reveal hidden problems. Estimate the cost savings or increased revenue that the customer will realize from the proposed project. To make it easier to sell the value, get the customer to participate in estimating the value.

- *Let your reputation speak for you.* Customers are willing to pay premium fees to top-notch service providers, such as IBM and McKinsey, because they are well known and respected in their markets. Invest in building your brand image with your target market. Services are sold on reputation and trust, and a strong brand helps establishes these qualities in the minds of your prospects.

- *Use success stories and references.* Share stories about the value you created for other customers—reduced IT costs, increased IT staff productivity, improved user productivity. Draw attention to quantifiable results that show your contributions to the bottom line. If possible, share business case studies that provide an in-depth analysis of another customer's key challenges, your solutions, and the business value delivered to that customer through your solutions.

- *Appeal to personal goals.* The project's executive sponsor may have much to gain or lose based on the success or failure of the project. Identify these personal goals, such as career advancement or bonuses, and point out how the project may result in praise, recognition, cost savings, or other benefits that contribute to these personal goals.

Customers want to maximize value and minimize price. If the customer asks for a lower price, then accommodate the request by reducing the scope of the service, transferring activities to the customer team, or replacing your senior consultants with junior ones. This keeps the conversation focused on value. If you don't focus

TABLE 14.1   Pros and cons of T&M versus fixed-price contracts

Time and Materials	
Pros	<ul><li>Service provider paid for the hours worked</li><li>Service provider does not incur risk if the project runs longer than anticipated</li><li>Less time required to scope/estimate project</li></ul>
Cons	<ul><li>Customer may haggle over hourly rates</li><li>Customer may dispute the number of hours worked</li><li>Customer doesn't know upfront what the project will cost</li><li>Project may be cancelled if there is a company freeze on contractors</li></ul>
Fixed Price (cost-based, value-based, or market-based pricing)	
Pros	<ul><li>Customer knows total cost upfront (unless project scope changes)</li><li>Service provider is guaranteed fixed amount, even if project is completed quickly</li><li>Investments in methods, tools, and consultant training to speed service delivery may be captured by pricing the service based on value</li></ul>
Cons	<ul><li>Service provider incurs risk of project running longer than estimated</li><li>Customer may doubt that the service effort warrants the price</li></ul>

on value, you will most likely find yourself in a conversation about discounting hourly rates. Deep discounting can turn a Rolex into a Timex. Don't let discounting negatively affect your brand and your ability to deliver quality solutions.

To evolve your pricing from time and materials to cost-based or value-based pricing, keep close track of the hours you spend on major activities and deliverables for each project. As you document the efforts expanded, you will gradually build the skills necessary to provide a fixed project price. Of course, fixed price does not mean that your team may be working at no charge for endless hours. The better you do at creating a detailed work breakdown structure and managing scope creep with good change control procedures, the less likely you will incur project overruns. Be sure your contract includes the hourly rate that you will charge if the scope of the project increases.

Market-based pricing. Market-based pricing requires gathering competitive data and setting rates and fees based on competitive prices. However, competitive pricing information for professional services is difficult to obtain. Companies do not usually publish their hourly rates unless their primary market is consumers. Some companies have a wide range of prices for various skill levels of consultants and promote their average price. Periodically, market research companies, such as Information Technology Services Marketing Association (ITSMA), do studies that compare pricing practices of professional services organizations. If your company participates in the study, the results are usually provided for free. Otherwise, interested companies can purchase the report. These studies provide aggregate information on pricing policies and practices; they do not release individual price lists.

The summary report for a pricing study published by ITSMA includes the following quote from Julie Schwartz, vice president of research for ITSMA:

> "Most service providers are reducing prices rather than building value: many are competing as though their services are commodities. The reality is that price is rarely a key driver of the services purchase. Customers are not looking for commodities—they are looking for business benefits and return-on-investment. Marketing and salespeople must focus on communicating the value that their services provide." [15]

---

15. ITSMA Professional Services Pricing Study: Pricing Practices 2001, www.itsma.com/research/abstracts/PSS001.htm

Match Supply with Demand

Effective resource management is an essential element of any business. It requires understanding demand so you can provide products or services to customers when and where needed. Inaccurate forecasts can result in delay or inability to deliver the goods, or excessive capacity or inventory. In either case, misjudging demand impacts profitability. Let's look at how resource management differs for product and services businesses, and how you can improve your ability to balance supply and demand.

Products vs services. All product-centric companies understand and value capacity planning and capacity management. However, what it means and how it is managed for professional services is different from products.

Products. If a company sells more widgets than it planned one month, no problem. Product companies know how to crank out more widgets to meet an increase in demand. They find ways to speed up production, add another production shift, or hire more workers. It takes some effort, yet it is a problem that most companies welcome and can readily address.

Professional services. Now consider a situation where you need more consultants who are experts in Web services to architect a leading-edge solution. That opportunity cannot be addressed so easily. If demand is too high, a professional services manager can't simply add another shift to crank out more consultants with the required expertise. When consultants with the appropriate skill sets are not available to staff projects, engagements get delayed or even lost. There is risk in frustrating customers who requested the services, and risk in frustrating salespeople who are counting on these services to close a product sale. On the other hand, if a company hires too many consultants and ramps up too quickly, it may end up with an oversupply of consultants sitting on the bench while labor costs are impacting profits.

Monitor supply and demand. Because managing supply/demand is critical to the success of the business, it needs to be closely monitored. Successful organizations discuss both sides of this ratio at regular weekly meetings: (1) resource availability and (2) project backlog/forecasts.

By looking ahead, you can anticipate staffing requirements, understand who will be available to fill the roles, and foresee any skill gaps. Likewise, you can see shortfalls in sales. Whether the issue is lack of resources or lagging sales, don't get blindsided by the situation. Plan ahead.

Improve forecasts. To anticipate resource needs, sales teams must provide accurate weekly forecasts. Who are current prospects? What is the probability of winning deals? For each opportunity that has a high probability of closing, when will the engagements begin? Where are they located? What resources are needed to staff the engagements? What skill sets or level of expertise are required for each role?

If your company is launching a new product or increasing its sales in a particular product line, determine if you need to train or hire consultants with the skills to deliver related consulting engagements.

Know talent availability. To allocate staff to upcoming engagements, you must know all your consultants' skills sets and availability. Who is on the bench? Who will complete a project soon? What skills do these employees have?

At the same time, think about your staffs' interests. Some consultants may want to develop new competencies or skill levels to further their career. Consider staff interests, career goals, scheduled classes, desire to travel, and current utilization levels.

Demand exceeds supply. If the backlog is consistently strong, managers may need to hire or call on partners to meet the demand.

Build bench strength. In professional services, your biggest assets are your consultants. You want to hire the best and the brightest—people who have strong skills and experience in your particular competencies.

Scurrying around to fill key roles in an engagement that starts next month or next week simply will not produce the best results. Just as you build a sales pipeline to create smooth engagement flow, create a pipeline of qualified candidates whom you can draw on when needed. By identifying qualified candidates and building relationships early, you can act quickly to staff upcoming engagements.

Call on partners. Teaming with partners is a common approach for managing supply and demand. When you need an expert with a specific skill set—and one of your team members is not available—look at the resources in your skills database. Consider potential candidates' level of competency, prior work performed for your organization, location, and industry experience (if applicable). When you find a consultant who meets your criteria, check out her availability. On the other hand, if you have consultants sitting on the bench, see if your partners can use them on their consulting engagements. In either case, it requires that you invest in building effective partner programs and, if necessary, training a partner's staff on your processes and product line. (Partner programs are discussed in Chapter 13.)

Supply exceeds demand. If the backlog remains weak, sales need to increase or staff needs to be reduced. Before reducing staff, consider:

Maximize consultant productivity. By closely monitoring project forecasts, backlog, and consultant availability, you can maximize consultant productivity. When the backlog is weak and consultants are sitting on the bench, make your resources available to assist with presales activities. Consultants who are not working on billable projects or sales support can contribute to services tools and processes to improve the overall efficiency and quality of services delivery. With close attention to availability, you can better coordinate training.

Redeploy staff. Think carefully about the loss of knowledge, the costs to refill the position, and the impact of employee loyalty and morale, before resorting to layoffs. If you need to reduce staff, check into redeploying talent to engineering or other areas of the company.

Unfortunately, given the ups and downs in the economy, terminating staff is sometimes necessary.

Failure to match supply with demand well can result in loss of business and/or reduced profits. Effective resource management provides the equilibrium that is a key success factor in the PS business.

Measure Financial Performance

PS leaders need to determine the metrics that they will use to run their business. You need to consider:

- What to measure (revenue, bookings, turnover rates, bill rate)
- Whose performance to measure (consultant, project, practice, PS organization)
- How often to measure (monthly, quarterly, yearly)
- What metrics are most critical to achieve the organization's goals

The key metrics will vary by organization. However, there is one metric that *all* PS organizations will agree is important, and that is utilization, an important measure of employee productivity.

Utilization rate. Utilization is a key metric for measuring the performance of any professional services business. It tells you how much of your organization's capacity is being spent on revenue-producing work. It is measured as a percentage of how many hours are spent working on billable projects versus the total time available to work on projects.

Utilization rate per consultant = Total billable hours / Hours available for billable work

Utilization rate for organization =

　　Total billable hours / Hours available x Number of billable employees

---

Hours available is usually based on a 40-hour week less time allocated for company holidays and vacations. You may also want to factor in time for training.

Benchmarking and best practices in the computer consulting industry suggest using a utilization rate of 75 percent (30 billable hours per week) as a good target. However, during the first six to nine months after launching a PS business, the utilization rate may be as low as 50 percent while new consultants are getting up to speed. Also keep in mind that overtime hours increase the utilization rate and could result in an individual utilization rate of over 100 percent.

Information Technology Services Marketing Association's (ITSMA) summary report for its 2001 pricing study noted that utilization rates for study participants averaged 69 percent in 2001, up slightly from 66 percent in 2000. When comparing your utilization with other companies, recognize that utilization calculations may vary depending on whether hours devoted to internal projects, sales support activities, personal time off, and other non-billable hours are included or excluded from the total hours available (the denominator in the utilization formula).

Clearly, the more consultants "on the bench"—not working on a customer-billable project—the lower your organization's utilization rate. The difference of a few percentage points—for example, from a 70- to 75-percent utilization rate—can have a huge impact on your profit margins. On the other hand, a utilization rate beyond 85 percent is not realistic because consultants need time between engagements for training, company meetings, and other activities. Setting the bar too high can result in consultant burnout and turnover.

If non-billable duties such as presales support are an essential part of a consultant's job, treating the work as downtime can deflate your organization's utilization rates and diminish the importance of the work. To get a more accurate figure, factor out presales support from utilization to increase the likelihood that consultants will be made available for sales calls. Be sure your company has a consistent understanding of how utilization is measured.

TABLE 14.2 Key financial measures for professional services
organizations

Metric	Definition
Bookings	Funds expected from customers based on signed professional services contracts
Billings	Value of completed work that can be billed
Backlog	Value of contracts that have been received but are not completed (bookings minus billings)
Revenue	Total amount of money received for professional services (before expenses are subtracted)
Revenue per practice	Revenue recognized for individual practices
Net profit	Profit before tax (total revenue less all costs)
Gross margin	Measure of profitability (services revenue – cost of services) (divide by services revenue to obtain gross margin percent)
Utilization per consultant	A consultant's time spent on billable work (billable hours/ hours available for billable work)
Utilization	An organization's capacity spent on billable work (billable hours/ hours available x number of billable employees)
Realization rate	Percentage of dollars actually received for services compared to the total dollars that should have been generated based on list prices
Cost of sales	Total costs for selling professional services, including salaries, commissions, and other sales expenses
Sales proposal hit ratio	Revenue from proposals won divided by the potential revenue from proposals submitted

In order to optimize utilization, you need to accurately forecast and scope engagements so you can project the number of engagements and the number of hours each project will consume. You also need to consider employee skills in order to slot the right people into a project. It is possible to have a low utilization rate *and* a large backlog. This means that you don't have the staff with the skills needed for your business. In this case, you need to change the skill mix to match customer engagement needs.

Other key measures. Bookings, billings, backlog, revenue, gross margin, profit, cost of sales, and more (see Table 14.2) are other key measurements for a professional services organization. For additional information on performance metrics, check out Thomas E. Lah's book *Mastering Professional Services*[16] or Jenne Urich's Web-based article *Killer KPI's for Professional Services: Key Performance Indicators (KPIs) that Drive Productivity and Profits.*[17]

The goals for each of your financial performance measures will vary based on your mission and the maturity of your organization. During the first few years, a human-capital-intensive business needs to hire consultants and train them, establish a customer base, and build a services infrastructure. It is most important that the team is building referenceable customers—the profits will come later. Likewise, if the business model of your PS organization is to support product sales and drive product revenue, your goals for revenue, utilization, and other measures will be lower than if your mission is to maximize services revenue. However, if your company's services strategy is to become a services-led business, the PS organization needs to reach a higher level of profitability. Be sure your PS plan contains clear goals that are aligned with the corporate mission and product goals and is understood by all key stakeholders in your company. This is critical in order for your financial performance to be evaluated appropriately.

---

16.   Thomas E. Lah, *Mastering Professional Services*, Westerville, Ohio: Professional Services Press, 2005.
17.   Jeanne Urich, Killer KPIs for Professional Services, (2008) http://www.spiresearch.com/downloads/KillerKPIs.pdf

Automate Your PS Business Operations

In the 1980s and 1990s, professional services organizations had to build their own processes and software to manage their business. As Enterprise Resource Planning (ERP) has evolved to provide off-the-shelf software to coordinate all the resources, information, and activities for business processes, professional services organizations finally have software to manage engagements and their overall business. Professional Services Automation (PSA) software can help you schedule resources, track project status, manage time and expenses, manage project profitability, streamline overall financial project management, and more. You will find many alternatives to choose from on the Web.

Summary

Professional services leaders need to balance customer, employee, and partner responsibilities, while effectively running operations and ensuring revenue and cost are in alignment. If possible, hire managers with experience managing a PS business in another company or promote managers from within your own PS organization. Leaders from the product side of the business or from consulting firms face a considerable learning curve.

When pricing your services, consider that price is an indicator of quality, and avoid pricing your services too low. Determine whether you will price your services by time and materials expended or by providing a custom quote. Many professional services organizations start with hourly rates and then move to value pricing as they build their brand and become more experienced in scoping projects.

Select the appropriate measurements to monitor and manage your financial performance. Utilization is a key metric for all PS organizations. You can only make a profit if your resources are generating more revenue than they cost.

Questions for Consideration

Do your professional services managers effectively manage the business operations?

Professional services managers must establish effective pricing strategies and meet growth, revenue, and profit goals. Here are some topics for consideration to evaluate your business operations.

- Do your professional services leaders understand the dynamics of a product-centric business?
    - Do they have a good relationship with product executives?
    - Are they respected and valued by sales managers?

- How are your services priced?
    - Are most engagements fixed-price or time and materials?
    - Do you provide some services for free or discount your services?
    - Are your fees competitive?

- How well does your organization manage the supply/demand balancing act?
    - Do you have a well-defined process to ensure that you can both meet utilization goals as well as staffing needs?
    - Does your sales team provide accurate forecasts?
    - Are too many consultant hours spent on the bench?
    - Is time spent on product presales support impacting utilization rates?

- How do your rate your organization on setting and managing utilization targets?
    - What is your utilization target?
    - What is your quarterly and yearly utilization rate?

- o   How well does your utilization target match your services mission?
- o   What processes do you employ to manage utilization?
- o   How effective are you at meeting your utilization targets each quarter?

- What are the key financial measurements your PS managers use to monitor and manage the business?
  - o   How effective are these metrics in running the business?
  - o   What additional measures are needed?

- Do you have PSA software to help you run your business?

15

Bring It All Together

You need sound business strategies, methods, and practices to successfully manage and grow a PS organization in a product-centric company—and they are different from those of your product business.

The goal of this book was to help you *think* professional services. **Part I** discussed how selling and buying a service are different from selling and buying a product, and the factors necessary to win in the services game. **Part II** presented effective strategies to launch and manage a professional services business; and operational practices to market, sell, productize, and deliver professional services and manage partner relationships.

In this final chapter, we summarize the similarities in product and services business fundamentals, followed by a review of the unique aspects of professional services and some of the inherent issues that must be addressed by management.

It's about the Fundamentals

Let's not forget that the fundamentals of good business management apply to both product and services businesses. Both require clear strategies to manage the business effectively. These include the following:

- Aligning mission and goals with the corporate mission
- Defining a financial business model
- Balancing consistency across the organization and individual autonomy for local practices
- Targeting the appropriate markets and their needs
- Shaping and promoting a brand image
- Establishing core competencies and packaged products
- Building optimal sales organizational structure and sales techniques
- Hiring, motivating, and retaining the best people
- Maintaining and measuring consistent quality
- Defining the role of service partners

Both product and services organizations require an investment in an infrastructure to support the business including: finance and accounting, legal, sales, and marketing. And both require an investment in methods and procedures to achieve maximum efficiency, reduced costs, and consistent quality.

The difference between product and PS businesses lies in the content of the strategies and operational practices. Many product companies fall short by either failing to implement good business strategies and operations for their services business, or assuming that what works for the product business will work for services.

What's Unique about PS?

The premise for this entire book is that the nature of the professional services business within product-centric companies differs from the product business. So it seems fitting to end the book with a summary of the key distinctive characteristics of a professional services organization and their implications for the business.

Intangible "products." Professional services are produced *after* they are purchased. So the customer must trust that the PS delivery team will deliver results that meet his expectations. To be successful, customer expectations must be well defined in the statement of work, and the project must be well managed to ensure the deliverables are produced on time, within budget, and with high quality. Regular project meetings and project reviews, acceptance of deliverables, and issue- and risk-management processes are needed to ensure the customer gets what he anticipated.

Customization. Most professional services require some degree of innovation or customization. Because of this, the salesperson needs the skills and knowledge to understand each customer's unique challenges and to describe potential solutions. If those skills are not part of the rep's talent set, he needs access to technical resources who can assist with the sales effort. The custom nature of services also significantly impacts service delivery. The greater the departure of a solution from any other service provided in the past, the less the PS delivery team can rely on standard methods and sample deliverables.

Close customer interaction. To sell most high-ticket offerings, personal interaction with the customer is always important—but even more so with professional services. To sell professional services, face-to-face meetings with the customer are usually required. Because services are intangible and built after the sale, the sales team must establish a level of trust with the prospect. The trust is built on personal relationships, as well as technical competence and customer testimonials. Establishing trust usually requires a longer sales cycle than is standard for products.

Typically, professional services are delivered at the customer facility. Close cooperation with the customer is required in order to understand requirements and the current environment. The PS team often works side-by-side with the customer team to collaboratively implement a project. To successfully handle this high level of customer interaction, consultants must have strong interpersonal skills, as well as expertise in the specific competency required for a project.

Reliance on project teams. Professional services are delivered through projects teams. Managers, engagement managers, and other PS personnel must master the challenges of successfully winning projects, staffing them, managing them, and executing them. A team is formed to deliver a project at a customer site and then dissolved when the project is completed. A new team must be created to accommodate the needs of a new customer—just-in-time to meet his needs. This requires getting the right people to the right place at the right time—and doing this all cost-effectively.

Dependence on individuals. Although most engagements are delivered by project teams, there is also a high degree of reliance on the skills and experience of individual consultants to meet each customer's requirements. Engagement managers and consultants are constantly called upon to craft unique solutions, and exercise good judgment and decision-making skills during an engagement.

Difficult to ensure quality. The customer perception of the work performed during an engagement is the prime measure of quality. Customer debriefings at the end of each engagement and periodic customer satisfaction surveys provide valuable insights to evaluate the organization's performance and improve future engagements.

Geographically dispersed practices. Consulting practices are frequently scattered throughout a country or the world. Yet, to operate efficiently, consultants need to share knowledge, best practices, methods, lessons, and tools. A skills database is an invaluable tool to quickly find the right consultant for the job and maximize your resource utilization. A solutions database is crucial to capture and share the knowledge, or intellectual property, that is learned from each engagement.

Intangible services ... built at the customer site ... with a high degree of customer interaction ... usually requiring schedules and budgets to be set before the project commences ... with changes interspersed as the customer needs change ... and relying on individuals to exercise good judgment and decision making throughout the project—no wonder that professional services is a challenging business to manage.

Uniqueness Brings Challenges

Like any complex undertaking, there is no set formula for success when building a PS organization—just guidelines to steer you along the way. Every company is faced with the challenge of defining what is best for its own services business. The hard questions must be answered. How large? How strategic? How big an investment? What are the tradeoffs?

This last section will review some of the key decisions that PS management must address due to the unique nature of professional services in a product-centric company.

Mission. Establishing a well-defined mission is essential to the success of the PS business. The mission determines how your organization will be measured. It becomes the foundation for setting sales strategies, revenue and profit goals, and other business and financial strategies and plans.

What role does professional services play in your organization—strategic or tactical? Does professional services provide an entry into an account so products can be sold later? Or do products lead and professional services follow? Is the main goal of services to drive product sales or provide an additional revenue stream? Be sure to fully define your mission and objectives and get all key stakeholders to buy into it. Without a well-defined and accepted mission, your PS organization may be viewed as unsuccessful simply because it is being measured against the wrong business model.

Degree of autonomy. Because services are built at the customer site and usually require a fair degree of customization, the business requires managers and individuals who can respond to unique customer needs and make independent judgments and decisions. At the same time, customers come to expect a high degree of standardization from medium to large companies. Standardization becomes even more important for multinational companies who are looking to purchase similar products and services for its global offices.

PS organizations need managers who can implement creative solutions to problems. And yet, the organization benefits from economies of scale gained from standardized marketing materials, sales and delivery training, methodology, and business practices. Management must establish the appropriate balance between consistency across the organization and autonomy of practices or individuals.

Level of consistency in competencies and services worldwide. Because products are built in centralized corporate facilities, a company's product line is relatively consistent worldwide—with some variation to accommodate local preferences. The same degree of standardization is not automatically inherent in services. There is clearly some degree of differences among solutions because they are customized to meet each customer's needs.

Professional services organizations must decide on the degree of consistency in the competencies, markets, and industries targeted worldwide? If a packaged service is offered by the company, is it marketed in all locations worldwide? Can each local practice develop its own packaged services to market exclusively in its own geographical area? Can each local practice rely on its own unique competencies to offer solutions?

Investment in standards. When a new professional services organization is formed, it is dependent on the skills and experience of individual consultants. As the organization grows, it must consider how it can best leverage individuals to reduce costs and improve the quality of its solutions. It must also consider the degree of innovation required in the solutions provided to its customers. The higher the degree of similarity amongst projects, the greater the payoff that is gained from investing in standard methods and tools to deliver services. Each organization must determine how much it will invest in project management methodology, service delivery methodology, packaged services, and a solutions database to increase the efficiency and quality of its services.

Short-term vs long-term investments. Every company must consider how much it focuses on quarterly revenue gains versus investing in long-term growth. If your organization is faced with a decision about using your resources for a project that will greatly enhance the skills of the organization versus using your resources for a project that will provide significantly more revenue, which would you choose? Do you put your best consultants with top-notch specific competency skills on a project, or do you assign less-skilled consultants so they can develop their skills in the solution area—and assign the gurus as mentors?

The highest-quality methodology requires input from the consultants who are most skilled in the subject matter. And yet, these same top-notch consultants are consistently in demand for important engagements. Do you assign them to today's project, or do you make their time available to invest in the methods, tools, and training to assist other consultants in developing skills to enhance the global delivery of future projects?

Investment in solution selling. Selling services requires a different approach than selling products. There are training programs available to teach product salespeople a solution selling method. Unfortunately, even with training, a fair number of salespeople will not make the cut. At a services symposium several years ago, a presentation on selling services given by a technology industry analyst started with "fire your [product] sales team."

A PS organization must decide who is going to sell its services—the product sales team, a services sales team, business development managers, sales account managers with a PS overlay team, or channel partners. Will the professional services sales team report into the PS organization, the services organization, or the corporate sales organization? Will the company train salespeople—all or some—on solution selling practices? How fully will the company embrace the program for solution selling? What compensation programs will be implemented to provide incentives to sell services?

PS involvement in sales efforts. Practice managers, engagement managers, and other field personnel who are involved in delivering services are in the best position to help sell services. They have the best understanding of customer needs, the consulting process, and previous engagements. Every organization must determine how large a role these resources will play in the PS sales process. Of course, the dilemma is that the same resources that are needed to assist with sales calls are also needed for the revenue-generating activity of services delivery. It is strongly recommended that people who have a first-hand knowledge of PS engagement practices and prior projects—whatever their titles may be—be brought into the sales effort early in the process.

Partners. Every organization must decide the role that partners will play in selling and delivering its professional services. The worst error is typically not the result of a specific decision. Rather, it is the lack of strategy, plans, and processes for partner programs. Who is responsible for your PS partner strategy—your professional services organization, the channel partner and alliance organization, or both? What are your partners' expectations? How are the partnerships implemented and managed? How are partners goaled and measured? What is your strategy for dealing with a situation in which you and a partner are competing for the same services business in which your company's products play a key role?

Leadership. Every organization needs a leader with a clear vision. Who do you choose to lead the PS organization—an internal executive who knows your company, a managing partner of a consulting firm, or someone experienced in managing a PS organization for a technology vendor?

When I call a client whom I have not spoken with for many months, he usually shares with me the name of his *new* VP of Professional Services. The degree of turnover in this role reflects the challenging nature of this position. It requires someone who understands the unique nature of the professional services business and also has the skills to interface with the executives who "speak" products. An executive in a consulting firm typically spends a great deal of time interfacing with customers and assisting in the sales process. And yet, executives for technology vendors typically spend a good deal of time focused internally—managing the business and interfacing with executives. Each PS manager must determine the appropriate mix of internal and external activities.

In Closing …

Professional Services: selling promises … creating custom solutions to unique technical and business problems … working as a team at customer sites … using resources that may decide to walk away with little notice … meeting *all* customer expectations … matching supply with demand … achieving revenue and profit goals. It is a complex business.

Developing a professional services business in a product company adds another level of complexity. All professional services managers must strive to win engagements, deliver outstanding customer service, attract and retain the best and brightest people, and achieve profitability goals. In a product-centric environment, PS managers must achieve these goals while building and sustaining alignment with the company's mission, strategies, values, markets, and products.

The Art of Professional Services was designed to help you understand the basic principles, strategies, and operational practices of a professional services business—and how it differs from a product business. Any art form starts with learning the basic principles (breath control and voice placement when singing, chord mastery when playing the piano or the guitar, brush strokes when creating a painting ...). And so with professional services, it takes experience applying the unique principles to refine the art.

Bibliography

Bosworth, Michael T. *Solution Selling: Creating Buyers in Difficult Selling Markets*. New York, NY: McGraw-Hill. 1995.

Gerstner, Louis V. Jr. *Who Says Elephants Can't Dance?* New York: Harper Business. 2002.

Kaplan, Robert S. and Norton, David P. *The Balanced Scorecard: Translating Strategy into Action.* Cambridge, MA: Harvard Business School Press. 1996.

Lah, Thomas. *Mastering Professional Services*. Westerville, Ohio: Professional Services Press. 2005.

Levitt, Theodore. *The Marketing Imagination.* New York, NY: Free Press. 1986.

Lowendahl, Bente R. *Strategic Management of Professional Service Firms.* Copenhagen, Denmark: Copenhagen Business School Press. 2000.

Maister, David H. *Managing the Professional Service Firm.* New York, NY: The Free Press. 1993.

Moore, Geoffrey A. *Crossing the Chasm, Marketing and Selling High-tech Products to Mainstream Customers.* New York: Harper Collins Publishers. 1991.